Dedication

To all the people who have ever found themselves stuck in an office filled with quirky characters and messy work habits —may this book remind you that even in the most chaotic situations, laughter, collaboration, and a little bit of organized chaos can go a long way. *~Kandice Merrick*

Preface

Have you ever stared at the abyss of your overflowing inbox, wishing you could just disappear into the void of procrastination? Or perhaps you've found yourself caught in the crossfire of office gossip, wondering how you ever ended up in the center of a workplace drama that makes soap operas look tame.

If you've ever felt the pangs of office chaos, then this book is for you. 'Wrangle the Wreckage' is an invitation to delve into the hilarious and sometimes painful world of working with colleagues who, let's just say, aren't exactly known for their organizational prowess.

This book is a love letter to the messy, chaotic, and often ridiculously funny side of office life. It's a reminder that even the most disorganized individuals can find a way to work together, learn from their mistakes, and maybe even find a little bit of humor in the process.

Introduction

Imagine a world where a simple office supply shortage could trigger a chain reaction of events that would make a reality TV show seem tame. A world where the mere mention of a potluck could lead to an epic battle of wills and culinary mishaps. This is the world we're about to explore in 'Wrangle the Wreckage.'

This book takes a lighthearted look at the realities of working with colleagues who, well, let's just say, thrive in the realm of "creative chaos." From the chronic procrastinator who sees deadlines as mere suggestions to the office drama queen who could spin a tale of woe out of a misplaced stapler, these characters embody the essence of workplace disarray.

As we journey through their adventures, we'll discover the hilarious and sometimes frustrating ways they navigate the treacherous waters of office politics. We'll see how their seemingly chaotic tendencies can actually lead to unexpected successes, and how even in the midst of their disorganization, they can find a way to work together towards a common goal.

So, buckle up, dear reader, because this book is a wild ride through the world of office chaos. It's a reminder that even in the most disorganised of situations, humor and teamwork can always prevail.

Introduction to the Office Chaos

The air in the office was thick with the aroma of stale coffee and unspoken tension. It wasn't that anyone actively disliked their colleagues, but rather, a strange, unspoken agreement existed amongst them—a silent understanding that the office was a place to do work, not make friends. You could call it a harmonious discord, a symphony of silent misunderstandings played out on a stage of shared cubicles.

There was, of course, the ever-present Ms. Martha Meadows, the office manager whose love for meticulous organization was rivaled only by her passion for gossip. Martha believed in a hierarchy of pens, color-coded file folders, and the importance of a crisp, ironed uniform, which she wore with the air of a seasoned warrior preparing for battle. Her desk, like a well-oiled machine, could withstand the onslaught of a hurricane, though occasionally, stray papers would flutter around the room like lost butterflies.

Next, there was Mr. David DeMille, the resident procrastinator, whose desk was a testament to the power of procrastination. Papers piled high, coffee mugs stacked like miniature skyscrapers, and a rogue banana peel that had mysteriously found its way under his keyboard. David operated on the principle of "maximum efficiency in the final hour," which usually translated to a flurry of frantic activity and muttered apologies as deadlines loomed.

Then there was Ms. Eleanor Evans, a whirlwind of energy and enthusiasm, a vibrant kaleidoscope of personality who saw the office as a stage for her own personal drama. Eleanor, with her penchant for embellished stories and an uncanny ability to find drama in the most mundane situations, could spin tales of intrigue out of a simple coffee spill. She was a walking encyclopedia of office gossip, a master of whispers and knowing glances, and a champion of the unwritten code of office politics.

These three, along with a colorful cast of other characters—including the perpetually optimistic Mr. Thomas Thompson, who believed in the power of positive thinking, and the stoic Mr. Robert Roberts, who remained steadfastly detached from the office drama—were all part of the fabric of this unique office. Their quirks, their habits, and their individual personalities created a chaotic yet oddly captivating ecosystem that, despite its flaws, had a peculiar charm.

The office hummed with a low-grade buzz, a background noise of typing keyboards, rustling papers, and the occasional muffled outburst from Eleanor, who had just discovered that the office's air freshener had been replaced with a new scent. The calm before the storm, as it were, was a fragile, delicate equilibrium, a constant dance between order and chaos, with the potential for the latter to erupt at any moment.

The tension was palpable. It clung to the air like a stubborn perfume, reminding everyone that the office was not merely a workplace but a battleground of unspoken expectations, hidden agendas, and conflicting personalities. Underneath the veneer of professionalism, a silent war raged, a war waged with passive-aggressive emails, stolen lunches, and the occasional misplaced stapler.

The office was a microcosm of the world outside, a miniature version of the human condition, filled with its own set of challenges, tribulations, and triumphs. The daily routine was a delicate dance of communication, collaboration, and conflict. And as the days went by, one could only wonder if the office's calm would hold, or if the storm brewing beneath the surface would finally unleash its fury.

For now, however, the calm persisted. The office hummed with a kind of nervous energy, a collective sense of anticipation that something, something big, was about to change. It was as if the office itself was holding its breath, waiting for the moment when its delicate equilibrium would be shattered. And that moment, like a slow-burning fuse, was getting closer with every passing minute.

Meet the Cast

The office hummed with a quiet, predictable energy. The fluorescent lights flickered, casting a sterile glow on the cubicles, each one a miniature fortress of paperwork, coffee mugs, and sticky notes. This was the realm of the "Wranglers," a motley crew of office dwellers who, for better or worse, shared a common fate: they were all employed by the same company.

The atmosphere was decidedly calm, a stark contrast to the whirlwind of chaos that would soon engulf them. It was the kind of calm that precedes a hurricane, the quiet before the storm, a deceptive sense of normalcy masking the brewing turbulence beneath the surface. The calm was almost unsettling, an unspoken agreement to ignore the cracks in the facade.

The atmosphere was punctuated by the rhythmic clacking of keyboards, the occasional hushed phone conversation, and the gentle hum of the office coffee machine. These were the sounds of ordinary office life, masking a reality that was anything but ordinary.

The "Wranglers" were a diverse bunch, each with their own unique quirks and idiosyncrasies. There was **Harold** , the chronic procrastinator, whose desk was perpetually littered with piles of paper, half-finished projects, and empty coffee cups. Harold was a master of delay tactics, a skilled practitioner of the art of the last-minute scramble. He reveled in the adrenaline rush of near-deadline chaos, convinced that he performed best under pressure.

Then there was **Samantha** , the office gossip queen, whose
knowledge of the inner workings of the company, along with
the personal lives of its employees, was almost superhuman.
Samantha was a master of the whispered word, a weaver of
tales both true and imagined. She thrived on the energy of
drama, her days punctuated by the thrill of a juicy new tidbit.

And let's not forget **Mark** , the meticulously organized
control freak. Mark's desk was a testament to his unwavering
obsession with order. Everything had its place, every file was
perfectly aligned, and every pencil was sharpened to a razor-
sharp point. Mark was a stickler for the rules, a champion of
order, and a constant source of irritation for those who dared
to deviate from his meticulously crafted systems.

Next was **Linda** , the perpetually upbeat optimist. Linda was
the office cheerleader, always ready with a smile and a
positive outlook. She saw the good in everything, even in the
most dire circumstances. Linda's sunny disposition was
infectious, a balm to the frayed nerves of her colleagues. She
was a walking embodiment of the "glass-half-full" mentality,
a beacon of light in the otherwise dreary office.

Rounding out the "Wranglers" was **Steve** , the tech-savvy
introvert. Steve was the office wizard, able to solve any
problem with a few keystrokes. He was a master of code and
a digital Sherlock Holmes, solving mysteries with the speed
of a supercomputer. Despite his quiet demeanor, Steve was a
vital part of the team, his knowledge and skills a vital
resource for the office.

The "Wranglers" were an odd bunch, a tapestry of
conflicting personalities and habits. The calm before the
storm was a delicate balance, a moment in time where the
office's eccentricities were masked by a thin veneer of
normalcy. But beneath the surface, the winds of change were

gathering force, and the storm was about to break. The "Wranglers" had no idea that their lives were about to be upended, that their peaceful routines were about to be replaced by an avalanche of chaos, and that the office they knew would be forever transformed.

Routine Disruptions

The office hummed with a quiet energy, a deceptive calm masking the undercurrents of chaos that swirled beneath the surface. It was the kind of calm that precedes a storm, a lull before the hurricane of deadlines, missed meetings, and forgotten responsibilities. Even the air seemed thick with anticipation, a tangible presence hanging heavy in the air like the smell of stale coffee and anxiety. It was a place where the smallest disruptions, the seemingly insignificant hiccups in the day, were harbingers of larger issues brewing beneath the placid facade.

One such disruption occurred around 9:15 am, when the office coffee machine, a sputtering, wheezing relic of a bygone era, decided to stage its daily protest. Its usual symphony of grumbling and gurgling gave way to a deafening shriek, followed by a plume of steam that billowed out like a miniature geyser. The room erupted in groans and sighs, the universal language of caffeine-deprived office workers.

The culprit, as always, was the overflowing coffee grounds bin. A single, misplaced scoop of coffee grounds had been enough to set off the machine's internal alarm system, a system that seemed to have a life of its own. This was not the first time this had happened. The machine's erratic behavior had become something of a daily ritual, a predictable disruption in an otherwise predictable routine. But this time, the disruption seemed to carry a different weight.

The office manager, a stern-faced woman named Ms. Harrington, rushed to the scene, a worried frown etched on her face. She surveyed the scene with a sharp gaze, taking in the steaming mess and the disgruntled faces gathered around the coffee machine. "Well, it seems like we have another coffee crisis on our hands," she muttered, her voice laced with a hint of exasperation.

Ms. Harrington, the office's self-proclaimed "master of order," was a woman who thrived on routines and predictability. Disruptions, of any kind, were anathema to her carefully curated world. She had tried everything to tame the coffee machine's rebellious spirit, from meticulously cleaning it every week to investing in expensive filters. Nothing, however, seemed to work. The machine had a mind of its own, a perversely defiant personality that defied all attempts to control it.

The coffee machine, in its own way, was a metaphor for the office itself. On the surface, it was a well-oiled machine, a place of productivity and efficiency. But beneath the surface, a current of chaos flowed, a hidden undertow of missed deadlines, misplaced files, and forgotten tasks. The office's calm facade was thin, fragile, easily shattered by even the smallest disruption.

As the coffee machine continued its protest, spitting out a thin, sputtering stream of lukewarm water, a wave of murmurs rippled through the office. The staff, as if sensing an impending storm, grew restless, their anxiety rising with the steam from the coffee machine.

"This is just the beginning," whispered Janet, the office's resident gossip queen, her voice barely a whisper. She leaned over to her co-worker, Bob, and with a conspiratorial glint in her eye, she added, "Just you wait, the real chaos is about to unfold."

Bob, a mild-mannered man who preferred peace and quiet to the office's constant drama, simply rolled his eyes. He didn't believe Janet for a second. He knew the office was a place of chaos, a land of mismatched personalities and clashing work styles, but he also knew that it was his job to navigate the terrain, to avoid the pitfalls and navigate the treacherous waters of office politics. He was a master at compartmentalizing, at separating his professional life from the chaos that surrounded him. He had a system, a carefully crafted set of routines and rituals that kept him sane and productive.

But even Bob, the office's resident Zen master, had to admit that something was different today. There was a sense of anticipation in the air, an unspoken tension that he couldn't ignore. The coffee machine's sputtering and wheezing was a mere prelude, the first tremor before the earthquake.

In the corner office, perched on his leather throne of power, sat Mr. Patterson, the CEO. He was a man of routine, a man who lived by the clock, and whose world was governed by a series of carefully crafted lists and schedules. He was a man who, in his own way, thrived on order and predictability. But Mr. Patterson, too, felt a strange unease creeping in, a subtle shift in the office's atmosphere that he couldn't quite put his finger on. It was the kind of unease that comes with the knowledge that the status quo is about to be disrupted, that the calm before the storm is about to give way to something much more chaotic.

The office, for all its outward appearances of efficiency, was a microcosm of life itself, a collection of individuals whose messy human behaviors threatened to disrupt the carefully constructed order of their world. It was a world where deadlines loomed, emails piled up, and coffee machines sputtered, a world where the smallest disruptions could set off a chain reaction of events that would leave no one untouched.

As the morning unfolded, the disruptions continued, escalating in both frequency and intensity. The office printer, a temperamental beast prone to paper jams and ink leaks, decided to join the coffee machine in its protest. It spat out a stack of crumpled paper, the pages jammed together in a tangled mess. The office's network, already slow and sluggish, decided to crash, leaving employees stranded, their screens frozen in a state of electronic purgatory.

The day was quickly spiraling out of control. Every minor inconvenience, every small glitch, every dropped email and forgotten meeting was a crack in the facade, a reminder of the underlying chaos lurking beneath the surface.

As the day progressed, the office's collective anxiety grew. The tension in the air was palpable, thick and suffocating, like a blanket woven from the threads of missed deadlines, forgotten appointments, and a growing sense of dread.

"This is insane," sighed Janet, her voice weary from the constant stream of disruptions. "I think the office is cursed."

Bob, ever the optimist, tried to remain calm, reminding himself of the routines and rituals that kept him grounded. But even he had to admit that the day was anything but normal. The disruptions were relentless, a relentless barrage of annoyances and setbacks that threatened to derail their day, their week, their entire lives.

And then, amidst the chaos, something unexpected happened. Something that changed everything.

The office, much like the coffee machine, was a seemingly calm and predictable entity, a well-oiled machine that ran according to its own set of rules and regulations. But beneath the surface, like the grumbling and gurgling of the machine, lurked a current of chaos, a simmering undertow of anxieties, frustrations, and hidden tensions. The office was a microcosm of life itself, a collection of individuals whose messy human behaviors threatened to disrupt the carefully constructed order of their world.

And it was in those moments of disruption, when the coffee machine sputtered and the network crashed, that the office's true nature was revealed. It was a place where the smallest disruptions, the seemingly insignificant hiccups in the day, were harbingers of larger issues brewing beneath the surface. The office, much like life itself, was full of surprises, some pleasant, some not so pleasant, but always unpredictable.

But the office, like the coffee machine, had a surprising resilience. It was a place where, despite the chaos, the everyday anxieties and frustrations, the constant stream of disruptions, the staff managed to adapt and survive. It was a place where, despite the coffee machine's daily protests and the printer's occasional tantrums, the office's inhabitants found a way to keep things moving.

For in the midst of the chaos, a strange kind of camaraderie had taken root. The disruptions, the daily annoyances and frustrations, had a way of bringing the office together, of forging a bond between the staff, a shared experience that transcended the individual and created a sense of shared humanity. The office was, after all, a collection of individuals with unique quirks, personalities, and work styles, but it was also a place where, despite their differences, they shared a common goal: to survive another day, to navigate the chaos, and to make it through, somehow, to the end of the week.

The Procrastinators Plight

The office hummed with a comfortable, predictable rhythm. It wasn't the kind of rhythm that would grace the charts, mind you, more like the slightly off-key, slightly out-of-sync rhythm of a group of friends who'd had one too many glasses of wine. But it was a rhythm nonetheless, a comfortable, familiar hum that lulled everyone into a sense of… well, not quite complacency, but something close. It was a rhythm punctuated by the occasional, unexpected burst of chaos, like a rogue coffee stain on a pristine white shirt or a power outage that plunged the entire office into an eerie twilight.

These bursts of chaos, though, were quickly contained. The rogue stain? Dispatched to the laundry. The power outage? A quick call to the IT department, and the office was humming along again in no time. It was a routine, a dance that had become so familiar, so predictable, that it was easy to forget that beneath the surface, something was brewing, something that would soon disrupt the hum and shake the office to its core.

At the heart of this impending chaos sat a man named Barry. Barry was not a man to be underestimated. He was, in fact, a master of chaos. A champion of the last minute. A self-proclaimed connoisseur of the art of procrastination. His desk, like his life, was a testament to this philosophy. It was a whirlwind of paper, a landscape of forgotten projects, a symphony of unreturned emails. The only thing missing was a siren wailing a warning of impending doom.

But Barry wasn't worried. He thrived on the adrenaline rush of the eleventh hour. The pressure, the stress, it fueled him. It made him feel alive. He was a man of the moment, a poet of the deadline, a maestro of the last-minute scramble. He had a knack for turning impossible deadlines into achievable goals, a talent for weaving miracles out of a tangle of tangled wires. And he'd do it all with a smile, a twinkle in his eye, and a nonchalant shrug that said, "Don't worry, I got this."

The rest of the office, however, did worry. They worried about the day Barry's magic would run out. They worried about the day the deadline wouldn't be met. They worried about the day the chaos that was Barry's life would seep into the office and turn their well-oiled machine into a sputtering mess.

They weren't wrong to worry. Barry was a ticking time bomb, a slow-burning fuse that was bound to ignite the office in a blaze of disarray. But for now, the fuse was still burning, and the office hummed along in its comforting, predictable rhythm. The calm before the storm.

The storm itself wasn't a sudden, violent tempest. It began as a gentle breeze, a subtle shift in the air. A few missed deadlines, a few misplaced reports, a few overly ambitious promises. The office, still caught in the comfortable rhythm of its routine, hardly noticed these subtle shifts. It was only when the breeze became a gale, when the small disruptions began to cascade into larger, more disruptive events, that the office truly began to feel the weight of the impending storm.

Take, for instance, the office coffee pot. A beacon of civility in the otherwise chaotic world of the workplace. For years, the coffee pot had been a neutral zone, a place where colleagues could gather, exchange pleasantries, and fuel their caffeine addictions. It was a microcosm of the office, a place where the rhythm of work and the flow of conversations intertwined.

But, as the storm began to brew, so did the coffee pot's woes. The coffee started appearing in the wrong flavors, the sugar packets mysteriously vanished, and the milk frother began acting up, churning out a frothy mess instead of the creamy perfection everyone had come to expect.

The office, still clinging to its rhythm, dismissed these as minor inconveniences. But the coffee pot, like a canary in a coal mine, was a sign of things to come. It was a small but ominous sign that the office's routine was about to be disrupted, that the storm was upon them.

And the storm, it was clear, had Barry's name written all over it.

The office, however, remained stubbornly oblivious. They were too busy clinging to the familiar hum, too distracted by the day-to-day routines, to see the storm clouds gathering on the horizon. They were too busy trying to ignore the occasional, unsettling rumble of thunder, too focused on the comforting rhythm of the coffee pot, to see the chaos brewing in the background.

Until, of course, the storm hit. It didn't come with thunder and lightning, but with a slow, steady drizzle of chaos that began to seep into every crevice of the office. It started with a missed deadline, a forgotten meeting, a lost file. Then, it escalated, with a string of miscommunications, a mountain of unanswered emails, and a series of panicked phone calls.

The office, finally shaken from its rhythm, began to panic. The comfortable hum was replaced by a cacophony of confusion, the familiar rhythm of the office became a frantic, chaotic dance. And at the center of it all, like the eye of the storm, sat Barry, still with a smile on his face, a twinkle in his eye, and a nonchalant shrug that said, "Don't worry, I got this."

But no one believed him anymore. They'd seen the havoc he wreaked, they'd felt the chaos he created. The office, finally awakened to the storm, knew that the calm before the storm was truly over. And the storm, it was clear, was going to be a doozy.

The office, like a ship caught in a hurricane, was now at the mercy of the storm. The walls were shaking, the windows were rattling, the coffee pot had gone silent. And Barry, the man who'd started it all, was still standing, watching the chaos unfold with a sense of detached amusement.

He was, after all, a master of chaos. A champion of the last minute. A self-proclaimed connoisseur of the art of procrastination. And he wouldn't have it any other way. The office, however, was about to learn that the art of procrastination, while exciting for the master, was a disaster for everyone else.

The storm had arrived, and the office was about to be wrung out, twisted, and tossed around like a wet washcloth in a spin cycle. The comfort of routine was gone, replaced by a disorienting whirlwind of chaos. And at the center of it all, was Barry, the man who'd brought the storm.

His colleagues, however, were not ready to be swept away by the storm. They were not content to be victims. They were, after all, office workers, and they were determined to wrangle the wreckage, to tame the chaos, and to bring order back to their world.

They were, in short, about to embark on a journey of chaos, a quest to conquer the storm that was Barry. And the journey, as it turned out, was going to be a wild one, a roller coaster ride of mishaps, misadventures, and maybe, just maybe, some unexpected victories.

The Office Drama Queen

The office buzzed with a peculiar energy that day. It wasn't the usual pre-coffee morning sluggishness, nor the frantic rush before a big meeting. It was a subtle, yet distinct, hum of anticipation, a low-grade current of unease that crackled beneath the surface of routine. It was as if everyone in the office had collectively sniffed the air and detected a faint whiff of drama brewing.

The source of this impending storm, of course, was none other than Ms. Beatrice "Bea" Butterfield, the office's resident drama queen. Bea was a walking, talking tempest of gossip, a human tornado of whispers and hushed secrets. She was, in a word, a gossip enthusiast. Her specialty was in the art of turning the mundane into the dramatic, of finding intrigue in the most innocuous of office events.

Take, for example, the case of the missing stapler. A simple, everyday office incident, one that most people would barely register, transformed into a full-blown mystery in Bea's capable hands. The whispers began within minutes of the stapler's disappearance, a faint, yet persistent current that rippled through the office.

"Have you seen it?" Bea would ask, eyes wide with a mixture of concern and excitement. "Gone! Just like that. Vanished into thin air. Who could have taken it? And why?"

A few of her colleagues, particularly those who were new to the office, fell prey to her theatrical pronouncements. They leaned in, eager to hear the latest developments, their expressions mirroring Bea's feigned concern. The whispers began, a low rumble that gradually grew louder, morphing into a full-blown storm of conjecture.

The missing stapler became a focal point, a catalyst for endless speculation. The possibilities were endless. Was it stolen by an office thief? Was it an inside job, orchestrated by someone seeking revenge for a petty office grievance? Or perhaps, as Bea liked to suggest, it was a sign of something bigger, a harbinger of impending doom.

The reality, of course, was far less exciting. The missing stapler was simply misplaced, its disappearance a mere oversight. It eventually resurfaced, nestled among the clutter of someone's desk, its absence barely a blip in the grand scheme of things. But for Bea, the stapler incident was just another feather in her cap, a testament to her ability to transform the mundane into the extraordinary.

And so it went, day after day. Each office event, each seemingly inconsequential happening, became grist for Bea's gossip mill. From the new coffee machine's mysterious "gurgling" to the late-night email from the boss, Bea found a story in everything.

But Bea's penchant for drama wasn't just about idle gossip. It was a way for her to assert control, to become the center of attention, to feel important in a world that, to her, often felt chaotic and unpredictable. She thrived on the buzz of her own creation, the palpable energy of anticipation that she cultivated around her.

There was, however, a downside to Bea's theatrics. Her constant pronouncements, her dramatic interpretations of events, had a way of turning the office into a stage for her personal performance. Her colleagues, many of them exhausted by her relentless need for attention, often found themselves caught in her whirlwind of gossip and drama.

They tried to avoid her, to keep their conversations to a minimum, to avoid feeding her insatiable need for intrigue. But Bea, like a persistent mosquito, was impossible to ignore.

"Did you hear?" she'd ask, her voice a conspiratorial whisper. "There's a new guy starting next week. Apparently, he's got a secret past. They say he's a real wild card. Can you imagine? I'm just so curious."

Her colleagues, rolling their eyes in unison, would politely nod, feigning interest while mentally preparing themselves for the next episode in Bea's never-ending drama.

Bea, oblivious to the groans of exasperation and the rolling eyes that followed her pronouncements, continued to weave her web of gossip, turning the office into a stage for her own personal performance.

But unbeknownst to Bea, a storm was brewing. It wasn't the kind of drama she could orchestrate, the kind she thrived on. This was a different kind of chaos, one that threatened to upend the entire office, a whirlwind of dysfunction that would leave everyone, even the drama queen herself, scrambling for cover.

Colleagues Unite

The office was a symphony of chaos, a chaotic ballet of misplaced files, forgotten deadlines, and ever-present coffee stains. It was a place where the sound of a ringing phone could send shivers down your spine, knowing that it could be anything from a frantic client demanding immediate attention to a coworker desperately seeking a "borrowed" stapler. And amidst this symphony of disarray, our heroes - well, maybe not heroes, but at least well-meaning individuals - were determined to bring order to the madness.

Their leader was Beatrice, a woman who, despite her name, was not blessed with an abundance of patience. Beatrice was a self-proclaimed "efficiency enthusiast," a title that was less an actual designation and more a coping mechanism for the constant state of disarray around her. She saw the office chaos as a personal affront, a messy rebellion against her meticulous nature. Beatrice's eyes, ever vigilant, scanned the office like a hawk, identifying every misplaced paper clip and uncapped marker as a potential disaster waiting to happen.

The team's resident procrastinator, Edgar, was a man whose mantra seemed to be "Why do today what you can put off until tomorrow?" Edgar was a master of the last-minute rush, thriving in the whirlwind of deadlines he created for himself. He had a knack for conjuring up elaborate excuses, his voice dripping with theatrical despair, to justify his procrastination. To Edgar, every task was an obstacle course, a daring adventure he would only tackle when forced to.

Then there was Penelope, the office drama queen, a woman who could spin a simple "Good morning" into a three-act play, complete with villainous backstabbing colleagues and heroic last-minute rescues. Penelope's gossip was legendary, a network of whispered secrets that could spread faster than wildfire in a paper factory. She reveled in the drama, the intrigue, and the delicious thrill of being in the know.

And finally, we had Peter, the ever-optimistic office plant whisperer. Peter was a man who saw beauty in everything, even in the most mundane of tasks. He believed in the power of positive thinking, even when confronted with the most absurd situations. Peter's mantra was, "There's always a silver lining!" This, of course, meant that he often found himself apologizing for other people's mistakes, seeing the good in everyone, even when they were being, well, not so good.

One Monday morning, as Beatrice sat in her office, the mountains of paperwork on her desk seemingly multiplying before her eyes, she had a sudden epiphany. "Enough is enough," she muttered, clutching her head as if a migraine were brewing. "We can't keep working in this mess!" Beatrice needed a plan, a strategy to tame the chaotic beast that was their office.

She called a meeting, and as the team gathered, a mixture of trepidation and curiosity clouded their faces. "Okay, people," Beatrice declared, standing tall despite her anxieties. "We are a team, right? We have talents, we have skills, and we need to work together."

The team exchanged apprehensive glances. "Work together?" Edgar asked, his voice dripping with sarcasm. "You mean, like… collaborate?"

Beatrice glared at Edgar, ignoring his thinly veiled mockery. "Yes, collaborate! This is our chance to turn the chaos into…

order! We are going to take back control!" A collective groan emanated from the team.

"Beatrice," Peter interjected, his voice calm and soothing, "maybe we could just… work on being more mindful of our surroundings."

Beatrice shot him a withering look. "Mindful? Peter, this isn't a spa retreat. We need action! We need a plan!"

Beatrice, determined to save the office from itself, devised a series of elaborate schemes, each more ambitious than the last. There was the "Color-Coded Chaos Control" system, where every item, from staplers to sticky notes, would have its own designated color for easy identification. This, Beatrice insisted, would streamline workflow and eliminate time-wasting searches.

The team, weary of Beatrice's grand plans, reluctantly agreed to try. "We can do this," Penelope said, her voice dripping with irony. "We can totally implement a system where we color-code everything!" She leaned towards Edgar, her eyes twinkling. "Edgar, we can even make a chart of all the supplies. You can be in charge of the chart!"

Edgar, who was staring dreamily at a particularly interesting coffee stain on his desk, gave a halfhearted nod. "Sounds like a plan."

The "Color-Coded Chaos Control" system, predictably, was a colossal failure. Beatrice, armed with a rainbow of sticky notes and Sharpies, attempted to color-code every single object in the office. But as Beatrice's rainbow of sticky notes started to take over, Edgar, in a moment of "creative chaos," decided to "help" by adding his own artistic touch. He grabbed a handful of blue sticky notes and began to cover

the entire office in a sea of blue, even the poor office plants,
which looked like they were about to drown in sticky notes.

Penelope, ever the drama queen, found a new source of
gossip in the sticky note debacle. "Did you see the state of
the office?" she whispered to Peter, her eyes wide with mock
horror. "It's like a giant, sticky note explosion!"

Beatrice, in a fit of despair, abandoned her color-coding
dream. "Never again!" she exclaimed, collapsing
dramatically onto a stack of files. "Chaos will not be
defeated!"

The team, realizing the futility of Beatrice's color-coding,
decided to try another scheme. They devised a system called
"The Organized Chaos Agenda." This plan was more
focused and less reliant on sticky notes. It involved creating
a weekly schedule for all tasks, with designated time slots
for each person to address their own backlog of work.

Beatrice, still reeling from the color-coding catastrophe, was
hesitant. "A schedule? Is this really going to work?" she
asked, her voice tinged with doubt.

"We'll have to give it a try," said Peter, with his usual
optimism. "Maybe a little structure can help us all."

Edgar, in his typical procrastinator fashion, was already
thinking about how to sabotage the agenda. "I'll definitely
be too busy to follow this schedule," he mumbled, his eyes
fixed on a particularly interesting dust bunny under his desk.

Penelope, however, was intrigued by the idea of a structured
schedule. She saw it as an opportunity for a new kind of
gossip – gossiping about who was slacking on their schedule
and who was being the most productive. "We'll need to

make sure we're all on the same page," she said, her voice laced with subtle intrigue. "Or at least on the same page of the agenda."

Despite their reservations, the team decided to give the "Organized Chaos Agenda" a try. They each received a meticulously crafted schedule, complete with colorful charts, checklists, and time-tracking sections. The team felt a surge of hope, a belief that maybe, just maybe, this time, they could tame the chaotic beast.

But as with all good intentions, reality had other plans.

The first week of the agenda went fairly well. The team, spurred by a renewed sense of purpose, even managed to complete a few tasks within the allotted timeframes. The office, for the first time in ages, actually felt a little less like a hurricane had just swept through.

Beatrice, feeling a surge of optimism, even allowed herself to indulge in a tiny celebration – a single, meticulously ordered cup of tea. "This is working!" she exclaimed, her voice filled with newfound confidence.

The second week, however, was a different story.

Edgar, true to form, immediately found a loophole in the schedule. He started claiming that his "creative thinking" required him to "think outside the box," which involved spending hours looking for inspiration on his social media feeds. The rest of the team found themselves spending countless hours trying to pry Edgar away from his "creative process."

Penelope, meanwhile, saw the schedule as an opportunity to unleash her gossip-mongering tendencies. She meticulously tracked everyone's progress, recording every missed deadline and every delayed task. She then spread these "insights" throughout the office, using them as fuel for her ever-expanding web of gossip.

By the end of the second week, the office was back to its chaotic self. Beatrice, defeated, collapsed onto her chair, her dreams of a perfectly organized office crumbling around her.

The team, however, was not yet ready to surrender. They had a new plan, a scheme that would require teamwork, strategy, and a healthy dose of humor. They called it, "The Chaotic Symphony." This plan involved accepting the inevitable chaos of the office and using it to their advantage. They would learn to work with the chaos, not against it.

The journey to "The Chaotic Symphony" was not an easy one. It was filled with mishaps, misunderstandings, and an endless supply of coffee spills. But through it all, the team learned to laugh at themselves, to embrace the absurdity of their situation, and to discover the true power of teamwork, even in the midst of chaos.

The "Chaotic Symphony" would be their final act, their symphony of laughter, resilience, and a newfound appreciation for the quirky symphony of their work lives.

The Plan in Action

The plan was simple, deceptively so, almost embarrassingly straightforward. It was Brenda, the office's resident pragmatist, who'd had the epiphany. "We need to make chaos a little… inconvenient," she'd declared, her voice surprisingly firm for someone who usually flitted through the office like a hummingbird on a caffeine binge.

Their first target: the dreaded "Free Snacks" cupboard, a chaotic abyss of half-eaten cookies, stale crackers, and mysterious concoctions whose labels had long since been devoured by rogue coffee spills. Brenda's solution was elegant in its simplicity: a system. A system for choosing snacks, a system for replenishing snacks, a system for… you get the picture.

This involved colorful labels, a rotating schedule (Brenda, of course, insisted on creating a spreadsheet for that), and a designated "Snack Warden" for each day. The Snack Warden, in theory, would be responsible for restocking the cupboard with items approved by the office "Snack Committee."

The Snack Committee was Brenda's brainchild, a democratic assembly of office dwellers tasked with deciding which snacks were worthy of the "Free Snacks" cupboard. It was a noble goal, but unfortunately, the Snack Committee itself became a microcosm of the office's inherent chaos.

"What about these gourmet pretzels?" asked Miguel, holding up a box of pretzel twists that looked suspiciously like something he'd found in his grandfather's basement. "They're vintage! They have a history!"

"Miguel," Brenda sighed, her voice strained, "they have a history of being moldy."

The Snack Committee meetings devolved into a cacophony of opinions. The perpetually distracted Mark, who often wandered into meetings mid-sentence, argued for the inclusion of energy bars, "because we need to stay energized," while the perpetually stressed Claire championed the inclusion of dark chocolate "for mental health," a sentiment met with a chorus of enthusiastic nods from the rest of the team.

In the midst of the chaos, a lone voice of dissent emerged. It was Gary, the office's resident cynic, who, in his usual sardonic tone, declared, "This is all a big waste of time. We're just going to end up with a cupboard full of granola bars that nobody wants."

"Gary," Brenda countered, her voice tinged with exasperation, "the point is to establish order, not to achieve a perfect system."

"Ah," Gary smirked, his eyes twinkling with mischievous amusement, "so you're saying this is more of a performance art than a practical solution?"

Despite Gary's skepticism, the Snack Warden system was implemented. The cupboard, for a brief, shining moment, was a symphony of order. Each day, the Snack Warden diligently restocked the shelves, ensuring that only approved snacks were available. But then, as if cursed by some invisible hand, the system began to unravel.

The Snack Wardens, overwhelmed by the responsibility and the sheer volume of snacks, began to prioritize their own tastes. The once orderly shelves became a patchwork of haphazard arrangements. Bags of chips were scattered, granola bars lay in disarray, and the mythical "gourmet pretzels" were still lurking in the shadows, their mold spores whispering tales of forgotten snack committee meetings.

The Snack Committee, meanwhile, had descended into utter pandemonium. Their meetings resembled a chaotic ballet, with members dancing around tables, bumping into each other, and arguing over the merits of seaweed snacks versus gummy bears.

The initial excitement surrounding the new Snack Warden system had waned, replaced by a sense of weary resignation. The "Free Snacks" cupboard had returned to its former state of organized chaos, a testament to the office's inherent ability to defy even the most well-intentioned schemes.

But, in the midst of the snack-induced mayhem, a glimmer of hope emerged. The colleagues had discovered that even the most elaborate plans could be derailed by the unpredictable nature of their workplace. And, perhaps more importantly, they realized that even amidst the chaos, there was an undeniable camaraderie, a shared sense of humor that kept them going.

The first scheme, in all its glorious failure, had taught them an invaluable lesson: they might not be able to wrangle the wreckage, but they could certainly learn to dance with it.

Unexpected Outcomes

The initial plan, a masterfully crafted document filled with flow charts, color-coded sticky notes, and a spreadsheet detailing each colleague's assigned task, had been met with a mixture of awe and apprehension. The awe, of course, was directed at the sheer audacity of their undertaking. To think they, a group of ordinary office dwellers, had dared to challenge the very fabric of their chaotic workplace was a feat worthy of an office-wide celebration.

The apprehension stemmed from a more practical concern: the sheer complexity of their plan. It involved a meticulously orchestrated series of actions, all designed to nudge their colleagues toward a more organized existence. The idea was to gently, subtly, nudge them in the right direction, like a gentle breeze guiding a ship towards a calmer harbor.

However, as the plan was put into action, the gentle breeze morphed into a howling gale, tossing their ship about like a child's toy in a bathtub. The first casualty of the plan was the notorious procrastinator, a charmingly disheveled individual named Gary, whose office resembled an artistic explosion of crumpled papers, empty coffee cups, and half-eaten sandwiches. He had been assigned the task of organizing the office library, a daunting endeavor that required a level of discipline Gary simply did not possess.

The plan called for discreetly replacing Gary's beloved, yet hopelessly disorganized, filing system with a state-of-the-art, color-coded system that would bring order to his world. The idea was that the novelty of the new system would spark Gary's interest and inspire him to embrace a more organized approach. Instead, it sparked a firestorm. Gary, convinced that the new system was an elaborate prank, retaliated by hiding the office coffee machine, a move that plunged the office into a caffeine-induced meltdown.

The drama queen of the office, a woman named Brenda, who could find a reason to be offended by the mere presence of a stapler, was assigned the task of organizing the office pantry. Her notorious gossip mongering was to be redirected towards spreading the gospel of a well-stocked and organized pantry, where snacks were neatly labeled and teabags were never left scattered on the counter. The plan was to use her natural inclination for drama to create a spectacle of order, inspiring her colleagues to follow suit.

But Brenda, in a dramatic display of misplaced priorities, decided to take the "pantry drama" to a whole new level. She began staging elaborate, impromptu fashion shows in the pantry, using the office's stash of snacks as props and costumes. The pantry, once a haven of quick breakfasts and afternoon energy boosts, transformed into a runway for Brenda's outrageous pronouncements on the latest trends in office attire, which invariably included a critique of her colleagues' fashion choices.

The plan, which had been so carefully crafted, so full of hope and optimism, was unraveling faster than a poorly-made sweater in a washing machine. The carefully orchestrated nudges had turned into full-fledged pushes, and the gentle breeze had morphed into a tempest.

And as the office descended into a chaotic abyss, a sense of despair began to creep over those who had dared to dream of a more organized world. Their plan, their hopes, their dreams - all of it seemed to be crumbling around them like a poorly built sandcastle in a hurricane.

But even in the midst of the wreckage, a glimmer of hope remained. The colleagues, despite their initial despair, found a strange sort of unity in their shared misery. They began to see the humor in their disastrous situation, laughing at their own misadventures, their misguided efforts, and their attempts to restore order to a world that seemed determined to remain in chaos.

The office, once a breeding ground for tension and resentment, transformed into a haven for shared misery. And as they huddled together, their laughter echoing through the hallways, they began to realize that maybe, just maybe, they were onto something. Their plan may have been a disaster, but the chaos it had unleashed had brought them closer than ever before. They had found a common bond, a shared experience, a sense of camaraderie that transcended the chaos.

Their efforts to impose order had failed, but their efforts to find unity in the midst of the chaos had succeeded. They had discovered that sometimes, the greatest triumphs are not in achieving a perfect outcome, but in finding meaning and laughter in the midst of utter chaos. And so, as the office continued to spiral into a whirlwind of disarray, they knew that somehow, somehow they would find a way to not only survive, but to thrive.

They had underestimated the power of their colleagues' quirks, the tenacity of their resistance to change, and the potential for chaos to become their unifying force. But they had also discovered an unexpected strength within themselves, a resilience that allowed them to laugh in the face of adversity, a sense of community that emerged from the ashes of their disastrous plan. The office, once a symbol of disorganization, was now a testament to their resilience, a reminder that even the greatest calamities can sometimes lead to the most unexpected and rewarding discoveries.

Chaos Intensifies

The initial schemes, while well-intentioned, were a disaster. The "Organized Office Initiative," as they grandiosely titled it, aimed to combat procrastination, gossip, and general disarray. Their first target was the office's notorious procrastinator, Barry. They decided to create an elaborate "Procrastination Prevention Station," a brightly colored, overly-organized space with motivational posters, sticky notes, and an alarmingly loud timer.

They envisioned Barry, overwhelmed by the sheer organized chaos, would finally buckle under the pressure and become a model of efficiency. However, Barry, true to his nature, saw it as a playful challenge. He embraced the organized chaos, using the motivational posters as targets for his paper airplanes, turning the sticky notes into a game of "pin the tail on the donkey," and setting the timer to a hilarious, off-kilter rhythm.

Their next target was Denise, the office gossip queen. To curb her incessant chatter, they decided to implement a "Gossip-Free Zone," an area designated for quiet work. It was equipped with noise-canceling headphones, soothing ambient music, and a strict "no-gossiping" rule. Denise, however, saw this as an opportunity to reinvent gossip. She began whispering coded messages into her headphones, making elaborate hand signals, and even incorporating the soothing ambient music into her gossip narratives.

The "Organized Office Initiative" was meant to bring peace, but instead, it turned into a comedic symphony of unintended consequences. Barry's paper airplanes became a daily airborne threat, Denise's coded gossip spread like wildfire, and the office, instead of becoming orderly, became a playground of unintentional chaos.

The "Organized Office Initiative" was a colossal failure, but it wasn't all bad. It forced everyone to look at their individual and collective habits. It exposed their flaws and highlighted the need for a more collaborative approach.

During a particularly intense episode of office chaos, where Barry's paper airplane nearly caused a coffee spill and Denise's whispered gossip led to a misunderstanding, the office found itself in a state of disarray.

"This is a disaster!" shouted Sarah, the office manager, her voice rising above the cacophony of clanging coffee mugs and whispered rumors. "Our initial plan backfired spectacularly. We need a new approach. We can't keep fighting against chaos, we have to embrace it."

The office stared at Sarah, unsure if she was serious.

"Embrace it?" questioned Greg, the office accountant, his eyes wide with disbelief. "How can we embrace chaos?"

"We can't simply control it," explained Sarah. "We have to understand it. We need to find a way to work with our chaos, not against it."

The idea of embracing chaos was unsettling, but it was also strangely intriguing.

The office, for the first time, began to seriously analyze their individual contributions to the disarray. Barry, ever the procrastinator, realized his tendency to delay was not just a personal quirk, but a symptom of underlying anxieties about the workload. He began to share his worries with the team, creating an open dialogue about time management and support systems.

Denise, the office gossip, was finally confronted with the impact of her whispers. She realized that her gossip was not just harmless fun, but could be hurtful and damaging to others. She took a step back, using her communication skills for good, becoming a mediator instead of a rumor monger.

As individuals began to understand their own roles in the chaos, they found a new kind of unity. The "Organized Office Initiative" might have been a disaster, but it forced them to confront their own flaws and work together to find a solution.

The office started a new initiative, one that embraced their imperfections and learned to adapt to their chaotic nature. They started small, focusing on communication and compromise. The goal was to create a shared understanding of their collective challenges, and to develop strategies that worked for everyone, not just a few.

The "Chaos Collaboration" initiative, as they jokingly called it, was a slow process. There were moments of frustration, miscommunication, and occasional flare-ups of the old, destructive habits. But overall, there was a sense of progress.

Barry, the procrastinator, started to delegate tasks and prioritize his workload. He discovered that by sharing his anxieties, he found solutions that alleviated the pressure and made him more productive.

Denise, the gossip, found a new purpose in fostering a sense of community. She became a natural storyteller, sharing anecdotes and experiences that brought the team together.

The office, once a battleground of individual quirks, was slowly transforming into a space of collaboration and understanding.

The change was subtle, but it was real. The office became a haven of laughter, not just because of the chaos, but because of the shared experience of managing it. The "Organized Office Initiative" might have been a disaster, but it paved the way for a new kind of order – an order that embraced the unique personalities and quirks of each individual, creating a space where chaos was not a threat, but an opportunity.

The office, no longer afraid of the disarray, learned to dance with it. They learned to laugh with it, and even, in a strange way, to love it.

"See," said Sarah, the office manager, watching Barry hilariously navigate his way out of a paper airplane trap. "We're a team now. We may be messy, but we're in this together."

The office laughed, a collective, shared sound that echoed in the room. They were a team, indeed, a team of misfits, a team of chaos, a team that found strength in their shared imperfections.

The "Organized Office Initiative" was a disaster, but it was also a turning point. It was the moment when they realized that their chaos wasn't a burden, but a source of strength. It was the moment they learned to embrace the mess, and in doing so, they discovered a new kind of order, a new kind of unity.

A Moment of Reflection

The initial attempts to tame the office chaos had backfired spectacularly. The colleagues, who had once envisioned a harmonious workplace free from procrastination and office drama, found themselves knee-deep in a whirlwind of unintended consequences. Their carefully crafted plans, designed to coax their colleagues into order, had instead triggered a domino effect of unforeseen chaos.

"This is all a disaster," moaned Emily, the perpetually stressed office manager, her hands buried deep in her hair. "We're further away from order than ever before!"

"Maybe we need a new approach," suggested David, the resident problem solver, known for his unorthodox but effective solutions. "Perhaps instead of trying to control the chaos, we embrace it."

His words were met with bewildered stares.

"Embrace chaos? You're kidding, right?" gasped Susan, the chronic procrastinator, who saw chaos as her natural habitat.

"I'm serious," David pressed on, his eyes twinkling with a mischievous glint. "We're fighting against a force that's already deeply ingrained in this office. What if we work with it instead?"

The colleagues exchanged hesitant glances. The idea of accepting chaos seemed ludicrous, even blasphemous in the sacred space of an office. But David's persistence and the undeniable evidence of their failed schemes began to shift their perspectives.

"Okay," said Sarah, the office drama queen, her voice laced with a hint of doubt. "I'm willing to try anything at this point. But how exactly do we embrace chaos?"

David's eyes lit up. "We create a system that allows the chaos to flow freely, but with boundaries. We turn it into a controlled chaos."

A wave of skepticism washed over the room.

"Controlled chaos?" Emily scoffed. "That's an oxymoron, David."

"Think of it like a roller coaster," David countered. "It's exciting, it's unpredictable, but there are safety measures in place. We can channel this chaotic energy into something productive."

"But how?" asked Sarah. "We're not a circus act. We're supposed to be doing our jobs, not riding roller coasters."

"We're not talking about literal roller coasters, Sarah," David said with a chuckle. "I'm suggesting we use the chaos as a catalyst for creativity. We can turn these messy habits into opportunities for innovation."

He elaborated, outlining a plan that involved turning the procrastinator's last-minute frenzy into a series of brainstorming sessions, harnessing the gossip queen's insights into a creative marketing campaign, and utilizing the constant state of flux to encourage adaptable thinking.

The colleagues, while still apprehensive, were intrigued by the concept. The idea of turning chaos into a source of fuel for innovation seemed too good to be true. They had spent so much time trying to extinguish the chaos, but now David was suggesting they use it as a spark to ignite their creative potential.

"It's a risky gamble," warned Emily, "but desperate times call for desperate measures. I'm willing to give it a shot."

The others, encouraged by Emily's newfound boldness, agreed. They spent the next few days meticulously crafting their plan, finding ways to channel the office's unique brand of chaos into a productive force.

The journey wouldn't be easy. They knew they were entering uncharted territory, navigating a world of unexpected twists and turns. But they also knew that by embracing the chaos, they might just unlock a level of creativity and collaboration they never thought possible.

The office, once plagued by disarray, was about to undergo a transformation. The colleagues, once victims of their own messy habits, were about to discover a surprising truth: chaos, when properly channeled, could become their greatest ally.

The air crackled with a mixture of trepidation and excitement. They were stepping into the unknown, venturing into a realm where chaos wasn't a threat, but a potential source of innovation. They had a plan, a vision, and a shared belief: they could turn the wreck into something extraordinary.

As the sun set on the office, casting long shadows on the cluttered desks and unorganized files, a sense of shared purpose emerged. They were no longer just colleagues, but a team, united in their quest to tame the chaotic beast that had long haunted their workplace. They were ready to "wrangle the wreckage" and create something truly extraordinary.

Office Tensions Rise

The air in the office felt thick with tension, like a humid summer day that promised a brewing thunderstorm. The carefully crafted schemes that had been put in place to tame the office chaos were now unraveling, creating an atmosphere where every interaction felt like a minefield. It was as if everyone had suddenly realized that their efforts to create order had only served to exacerbate the underlying issues.

The first crack in the façade came from the ever-present drama queen, Sarah, who had been lurking in the shadows, her eyes constantly scanning for any morsel of gossip to fuel her insatiable appetite. As the stress levels escalated, Sarah had begun to weave her own elaborate stories, twisting facts and embellishing truths, creating a whirlwind of whispers that swept through the office like a dust devil.

One sunny afternoon, Sarah, in a rare moment of clarity, confided in her closest confidante, Olivia, a quiet and observant colleague. "I just can't stand it anymore," Sarah whispered, her voice barely audible above the hum of the office air conditioner. "They're all trying to control me, to silence me. But I won't let them."

Olivia, who had long suspected Sarah's penchant for fabricating stories, listened intently. Her demeanor remained neutral, but her eyes flickered with a hint of amusement. "They're not trying to control you," Olivia replied, her voice as calm as a still pond. "They're just trying to get things done. Maybe you're the one who needs to be a little more… organized."

Sarah's eyes narrowed. "Organized? Me? You're kidding, right? I am organized. I'm just… creative with my methods."

Olivia let out a soft sigh. "Sarah, you've been spreading rumors about everyone. You're creating unnecessary drama. It's time to stop."

Sarah's face flushed red. "I'm not spreading rumors. I'm just… sharing information. It's all true. Everyone has secrets. They're all hiding something."

Olivia shook her head. "No, Sarah. You're making things up. You're creating a toxic atmosphere. Everyone is stressed out enough without your… embellishments."

Sarah's eyes welled up with tears. "No one understands me. I'm just trying to make things interesting."

Olivia placed a hand on Sarah's shoulder. "Sarah, you need to stop. You're hurting yourself and everyone around you. Find a healthier way to deal with your stress."

Sarah stared at Olivia, her eyes filled with a mixture of anger and confusion. "You don't understand," she said, her voice choked with emotion. "I'm just trying to fit in. I'm just trying to be part of something."

Olivia felt a wave of sympathy wash over her. She realized that Sarah's need to create drama stemmed from a deep-seated insecurity, a fear of being left out. "I understand, Sarah," Olivia said gently. "But you need to find a different way to connect with people. You need to be genuine."

Olivia's words hung in the air between them. Sarah looked at her friend, a glimmer of understanding finally entering her eyes. "What do you mean?" she asked, her voice softer now.

"Just be yourself," Olivia said. "Be honest. Be kind. Be supportive. You don't need to create drama. You don't need to be the center of attention. You just need to be you."

Sarah nodded slowly, processing Olivia's words. A long silence stretched between them, filled with unspoken emotions. Finally, Sarah spoke, her voice small but resolute. "I'll try," she said.

Olivia smiled. "I know you will."

As Olivia watched Sarah walk away, she couldn't help but feel a sense of hope. Maybe this was the turning point. Maybe Sarah was finally ready to face her own insecurities and embrace the power of authenticity. But Olivia also knew that Sarah's journey wouldn't be easy. There were still many more challenges ahead.

And then there was the matter of John, the office procrastinator, whose chronic aversion to deadlines had become a running joke. While Sarah was the architect of the office drama, John was the catalyst for its amplification. He was a master of the last-minute scramble, a virtuoso of the impromptu panic attack. He thrived on chaos, feeding off the adrenaline rush that came with pulling a project out of the fire at the last minute.

As the office tension grew, John's chaotic tendencies only intensified. His procrastination became more reckless, his deadlines slipped further, and his pronouncements of "I'll get it done, just give me a few more minutes!" became more frequent. He had convinced himself that he worked best under pressure, that his last-minute bursts of creativity were what made him so unique and valuable.

But the rest of the office wasn't buying it. They had grown tired of John's antics, his constant requests for extensions, and his seemingly endless ability to delay. His colleagues began to resent him, seeing his procrastination as a burden, a constant threat to their own deadlines and productivity.

The situation reached a boiling point when John, with a deadline looming, announced to the office, with a disarmingly innocent smile, that he was going to take a "quick break" to "clear his head." The office erupted in a chorus of groans, protests, and a few choice words that would likely get John a reprimand if the office manager overheard.

John, oblivious to the growing resentment, headed to the breakroom, a place where he could procrastinate in blissful anonymity, surrounded by free snacks and the allure of the office coffee machine.

But John's escape was short-lived. He had barely settled into a comfy chair, a bag of chips in hand, when he was interrupted by the booming voice of his manager, Mr. Thompson. Mr. Thompson, a man known for his rigid adherence to deadlines and his disdain for anything that resembled chaos, was not amused by John's latest procrastination escapade.

"John," Mr. Thompson said, his voice laced with a hint of exasperation, "I'm not sure what you think you're doing, but this project is due in two hours. We're not waiting anymore. Get back to your desk. Now."

John, momentarily caught off guard by the unexpected intrusion, felt his heart sink. He glanced at the clock, his blood running cold as he realized the gravity of the situation.

His "quick break" had stretched into a lost hour, and now the deadline was breathing down his neck.

He threw the half-eaten bag of chips back into the break room bag, mumbled a quick apology to Mr. Thompson, and scurried back to his desk. His mind raced as he tried to assess the damage. He had left his work half-finished, his notes scattered, and his thoughts in complete disarray. He was in a full-blown panic mode.

The office, sensing John's impending meltdown, watched with a mix of amusement and pity. They knew that John's procrastination was a problem, but they also knew that he had a knack for pulling things together at the last minute. They were hoping, for their own sake, that he would find a way to pull it off again.

John sat at his desk, his fingers flying over the keyboard, his mind churning with ideas. He was in his element now, the pressure of the deadline igniting a spark of creativity. He tapped away with a frenzy, fueled by adrenaline and caffeine. He knew he had to push himself to the limit, to tap into his inner procrastinator's magic.

As the clock ticked down to the deadline, John felt a sense of accomplishment wash over him. He had done it. He had finished the project. He had, once again, pulled a rabbit out of his hat. He slumped back in his chair, exhausted but exhilarated.

But his triumph was short-lived. As he sent the final draft to Mr. Thompson, a wave of dread washed over him. He had, in his haste, forgotten to include a crucial section of the report. His heart sank. He had failed.

Mr. Thompson, a man who prided himself on his meticulousness, immediately spotted the omission. His eyes narrowed, his expression turning from a slight frown to a full-fledged scowl.

"John," Mr. Thompson said, his voice dripping with disappointment, "I'm not sure what's going on, but you've missed a major component of this report. This is unacceptable. This project is critical to our department, and you're jeopardizing the entire team with your irresponsible behavior."

John, his face pale and his heart heavy, could only offer a sheepish apology. He knew he had made a mistake, a mistake that could have serious consequences. He was now staring down the barrel of a professional disaster.

The rest of the office, watching the unfolding drama, held their breath. They knew that John's procrastination had pushed the team to the brink. And now, it seemed, the consequences were finally coming to light.

Uncovering Secrets

The air in the office was thick with tension. The first attempt at a scheme to clean up the mess had backfired spectacularly, leaving everyone even more stressed and the office in a state of utter disarray. It was a battleground of crumpled papers, overflowing coffee mugs, and abandoned lunchboxes. The very aroma in the air was a potent blend of stale coffee, forgotten tuna sandwiches, and a potent whiff of desperation.

Amidst the chaos, whispers began to circulate. Rumours of discontent, resentment, and hidden agendas spread like wildfire. The pressure cooker of the office was reaching its boiling point. The most dramatic consequence of the first scheme was a revelation that shook everyone to their core. The ever-present office gossip queen, the infamous Brenda, had been secretly orchestrating the chaos all along. Her meticulously cultivated persona of a friendly, helpful colleague crumbled like a stale pastry.

It was a moment of dramatic irony. The scheme to bring order to the office had revealed the root of the disorder - a rogue gossip with an insatiable thirst for drama. Brenda, a master of the subliminal, had subtly orchestrated the chaos by dropping subtle hints, planting seeds of doubt, and fueling the flames of office drama.

The discovery of Brenda's manipulative tendencies came to light through a series of unexpected events. First, a forgotten email, mistakenly forwarded, revealed a string of messages she'd sent to various colleagues, subtly undermining their work and turning them against each other. The email was a bombshell. The contents were a cocktail of veiled criticisms, fabricated gossip, and subtle manipulation. It was a testament to Brenda's cunning ability to manipulate situations and sow discord.

Brenda's facade of innocence shattered with each revelation. Her carefully constructed image of a harmless, friendly colleague fell apart, exposing the manipulative mastermind behind the chaos. The colleagues, initially stunned by the discovery, were then fuelled with righteous indignation. The office, once a breeding ground for Brenda's gossip, was now a battleground for truth and justice.

The revelation about Brenda's true nature came as a shock to all, even to the unsuspecting office newbie, Emily. Emily, known for her innocent optimism and unwavering belief in the good in people, was utterly stunned. Brenda, to her, had been the embodiment of kindness and helpfulness. Emily's faith in Brenda was absolute, and the betrayal cut deep. It was as if the very foundation of Emily's office experience had been shaken.

The revelation about Brenda also affected the office's most notorious procrastinator, Tom. He was known for his talent of turning even the most straightforward task into a chaotic odyssey. Tom, initially suspicious of Brenda's constant "helpful" advice, now saw her manipulative tactics as a direct affront to his own chaotic genius. His resentment towards Brenda took on a new intensity, tinged with an almost comedic frustration.

The revelation about Brenda, however, was not without its silver linings. It served as a catalyst for the colleagues to unite against their common enemy. Their individual grievances against Brenda took on a collective significance. They realised that Brenda was not just a source of gossip, but a threat to their overall well-being. The collective resentment, fuelled by Brenda's betrayal, became a binding force uniting the colleagues.

The office, once a playground of individual chaos, was now a united front against a common enemy. The colleagues, each with their unique quirks and personalities, now had a shared purpose – to expose Brenda's deception and bring her reign of terror to an end. Their plan was bold, risky, and, above all, highly unorthodox.

It was a plan that required cunning, patience, and a healthy dose of office politics. The colleagues, united by their shared disgust for Brenda's actions, devised a scheme to expose her, to dismantle her carefully built web of lies, and to reclaim their office from her clutches. It was a risky plan, fraught with uncertainty, and potential for backfires. But they were determined to reclaim their office, their peace of mind, and their sanity.

The revelation of Brenda's true nature created a shift in the office dynamics, forcing everyone to reassess their loyalties and alliances. It was a defining moment, a turning point that would forever alter the landscape of their workplace.

And it was all thanks to a single, forgotten email.

The Gossips Downfall

The office buzzed with a nervous energy, a palpable tension that clung to the air like static. It was the aftermath of the "Great Coffee Caper," a disastrous attempt to inject some order into the office's chaotic routine. The scheme, spearheaded by the ever-optimistic Emily, had involved a carefully crafted schedule of coffee breaks, designed to encourage productivity. The result? A series of missed deadlines, frantic scrambling, and enough spilled coffee to float a small boat.

The gossip queen, Veronica, relished the drama. She'd reveled in the chaos, weaving elaborate tales of sabotage and betrayal, her whispers reaching every corner of the office. But Veronica's reign of gossip was about to come to an abrupt end. The whispers had reached Emily's ears, and she was not a woman easily ignored.

Emily had always admired Veronica's social skills, her ability to weave through the office landscape, leaving a trail of information in her wake. But Emily was also a fierce protector of her team, and Veronica's gossipy ways were starting to erode the fragile unity they'd built. Emily decided to take matters into her own hands.

One afternoon, she found herself cornering Veronica in the breakroom. Veronica, sipping her latte with a practiced nonchalance, looked up in surprise. The usual playful banter was missing from Emily's demeanor, replaced by a steely resolve.

"Veronica, we need to talk," Emily said, her voice firm but measured.

Veronica, ever the social chameleon, tried to deflect the conversation. "About what, dear? Can't you see I'm busy?" she asked, a saccharine smile plastered across her face.

"I know about your little games, Veronica," Emily said, her eyes unwavering. "The whispers, the rumors, the fabricated dramas."

Veronica, her facade cracking, sputtered in defense. "Oh, come on, Emily, you're taking this too seriously. It's all just harmless fun," she said, her voice losing its usual confidence.

"Harmless fun?" Emily scoffed. "Veronica, your 'harmless fun' is tearing this team apart. You're spreading lies, fueling insecurities, and undermining everyone's efforts."

The blood drained from Veronica's face. For the first time, she felt a flicker of fear. Emily was not the naive, easily manipulated person Veronica had taken her to be. She was a force to be reckoned with.

"Emily, I'm sorry," Veronica mumbled, her voice barely a whisper. "I didn't mean to cause any harm. I just... I just like to talk."

Emily, her expression softening, sighed. "Veronica, we all like to talk. But there's a difference between sharing information and spreading malicious gossip. You've crossed that line. You've hurt people, and you've damaged our team."

The weight of her words hung heavy in the air. Veronica's gaze dropped to the floor, her eyes filled with a mixture of shame and fear.

"What do you want me to do?" Veronica asked, her voice trembling.

Emily met her gaze, her eyes filled with a quiet but unwavering resolve. "Start by being honest. Tell the truth. And start by apologizing to the people you've hurt."

The following days were awkward. Veronica, usually a whirlwind of social energy, seemed subdued. The office, once buzzing with her whispers, fell into an uneasy silence. But beneath the awkwardness, a sense of relief settled in. The constant tension, the insidious rumors, were gone. The office felt lighter, freer.

Veronica, however, found herself struggling. She'd always reveled in the drama, the power she held over her colleagues with her gossip. But now, without that power, she felt lost, adrift in a sea of uncertainty.

She found herself missing the camaraderie of the gossip circle, the thrill of sharing secrets and spinning elaborate tales. But she also felt a new sense of responsibility, a realization that her words had real consequences, and that the power of gossip could be both destructive and damaging.

One day, she found herself in the breakroom, watching Emily and the others. They were laughing, sharing stories, their faces lit with a shared joy. Veronica felt a pang of longing, a yearning to be part of that camaraderie, to be accepted, to be trusted.

Suddenly, a thought struck her. She had a chance to make things right. She could use her social skills, her ability to connect with people, to build bridges, to create a sense of unity. She could be a force for good.

Taking a deep breath, she walked over to Emily, her heart pounding in her chest.

"Emily," she said, her voice a little shaky, "I've been thinking. I've been a real jerk, spreading those rumors. And I want to apologize, to all of you."

Emily looked at Veronica, a flicker of surprise in her eyes.

"I know I can't erase what I've done," Veronica continued, "but I want to try to make things better. I want to be part of this team, to be a part of something good."

A slow smile spread across Emily's face. "Veronica," she said, her voice warm, "we all make mistakes. The important thing is that you're trying to learn from them."

Veronica, her heart swelling with a mixture of relief and hope, nodded. The path ahead was still uncertain, but for the first time, she felt a glimmer of optimism. The gossip queen was gone. In her place, stood a woman ready to embrace a new chapter, a chapter of honesty, kindness, and genuine connection.

Allies and Adversaries

As tensions simmered like a forgotten pot of coffee on the office hotplate, unexpected alliances began to form, defying the usual office hierarchy and cliques. The drama queen, once the undisputed queen bee of office gossip, found herself surprisingly aligned with the procrastinator, the very person she'd once criticized for his "lack of ambition." This unlikely pairing stemmed from their shared frustration with the office's latest organizational scheme, a "color-coded calendar" that seemed more designed to confuse than clarify.

"This is just…," the drama queen began, trailing off, her voice filled with a mix of bewilderment and indignation. "It's like they think we're all toddlers who can't tell green from blue!"

"Exactly," the procrastinator chimed in, his voice surprisingly animated for someone who'd spent the last week avoiding anything remotely resembling work. "It's all very well to have a system, but this one's about as helpful as a fly-swatter in a hurricane."

Their shared disdain for the calendar, a seemingly insignificant point of contention, proved surprisingly effective in forging an unexpected bond. They found themselves meeting in the pantry for clandestine "calendar critique sessions," dissecting the color-coding system and devising their own, more practical, color-coded replacements.

Meanwhile, the once-isolated team of spreadsheet enthusiasts – the office's resident data nerds – discovered a surprising affinity with the office artist, a free-spirited soul who'd previously been dismissed as "too creative for the real world." Their connection stemmed from a shared love of data visualization.

"You know," the spreadsheet whiz, a man who could analyze a spreadsheet in his sleep, said to the artist one day, "Your charts are actually pretty good."

The artist, who had previously been reluctant to show off his work to his less-artistic colleagues, was surprised by this unexpected compliment. "Really? You think so?" he asked, his eyes wide with surprise.

"Yeah, they're actually quite insightful," the spreadsheet whiz confirmed. "You know, if you could just apply a little more, you know, data analysis to them, they could be really powerful."

The unexpected collaboration resulted in a stunning series of data-driven visual presentations, which captivated the entire office. The spreadsheets became a work of art, with bar graphs and pie charts transformed into mesmerizing, dynamic displays of information.

Even the office manager, known for his rigid adherence to procedures, found himself drawn to the artist's innovative charts, the data coming to life in ways he never imagined.

This improbable alliance proved that even in the most chaotic of office environments, common ground could be found in unexpected places. It wasn't just about shared interests or skills, it was about a willingness to see past differences and appreciate the unique perspectives that each individual brought to the table.

The newfound alliances brought a much-needed sense of balance to the office, creating a more diverse and dynamic workplace where collaboration, not competition, became the norm. It was as if the office had finally found its groove, a rhythm that allowed everyone to express themselves and contribute their unique talents to the greater good.

However, this newfound harmony was not without its challenges. The drama queen, now aligned with the procrastinator, found herself increasingly conflicted by her loyalties. Her desire to be a "good" colleague often clashed with her innate need to stir the pot and gossip about the office's inner workings.

The office's resident cynic, a man who saw every meeting as an opportunity for a power play, found himself struggling to adapt to the new collaborative environment. His attempts to sow discord and sabotage the team's progress were met with resistance, as his colleagues were no longer willing to fall prey to his manipulations.

This shift in the office's dynamics brought a welcome sense of empowerment and unity, but it also exposed the deeper challenges that remained. The office was still a complex ecosystem of personalities, each with their own unique quirks and agendas.

The team, now acutely aware of the fragility of their newfound harmony, had to work even harder to maintain it. It was as if they had entered a new chapter in their office journey, one that required constant vigilance and a renewed commitment to understanding and supporting one another.

One evening, the office's resident tech guru, a man who could troubleshoot a computer glitch with the speed of a lightning bolt, found himself hunched over his keyboard, desperately trying to repair a server that had inexplicably crashed. The server was the lifeblood of the office, holding all of their critical data and files. Without it, the entire operation would come to a standstill.

As the tech guru frantically typed commands, the office's resident worrier, a woman who could find a problem in even the most mundane of tasks, paced nervously in the background.

"It's not working," she said, her voice filled with a mixture of anxiety and desperation. "I'm telling you, this is going to be a disaster."

The tech guru, normally unflappable, looked up from his screen, his face etched with concern. "Don't worry," he said, his voice calm and reassuring. "We'll get it fixed. It just takes time."

"Time? We don't have time!" the worrier exclaimed. "This is a catastrophe!"

As the situation escalated, the office manager, who had been known for his calm demeanor, lost his cool, barking orders at everyone to "find a solution, and find it now!"

The office, once a haven of calm and order, had transformed into a whirlwind of chaos, fueled by fear and uncertainty. The server crash, a seemingly insignificant technological glitch, had triggered a chain reaction of anxieties and doubts, threatening to unravel all the progress the team had made.

In the midst of the chaos, the drama queen, who had been busy gossiping about the latest office rumors, suddenly realized the gravity of the situation. She had always thrived on chaos, but this time, it was different.

This time, the chaos wasn't just a source of amusement or gossip. It was a real threat, a potential disaster that could impact everyone in the office.

"We need to work together," she announced, her voice surprisingly serious. "We can't let this ruin everything."

Her words, unexpected and heartfelt, resonated with the team. The office manager, still flustered but beginning to regain his composure, nodded in agreement.

"Yes, we need to work together," he said, his voice regaining some of its former authority. "We can do this. We are a team."

The drama queen, once the queen of office gossip, now found herself in a new role: a leader, a voice of reason in a storm of uncertainty. She took charge, coordinating the team's efforts, assigning roles, and encouraging everyone to work together to resolve the crisis.

The procrastinator, inspired by the drama queen's newfound leadership, shed his usual procrastination tendencies, embracing the challenge with surprising energy and focus. He dug into the server's documentation, his usual avoidance of responsibility replaced by a newfound sense of urgency and purpose.

Even the office's resident cynic, who had initially been skeptical of the team's ability to overcome the crisis, found himself swept up in the spirit of collaboration. He contributed his insights, his cynical commentary now tempered by a newfound sense of shared responsibility.

The office, once a battleground of rivalries and petty conflicts, was transformed into a united front, a team of unlikely heroes, all working together to restore order and prevent a complete meltdown.

The server, after a grueling marathon of troubleshooting, finally came back online. The office erupted in a wave of relief and gratitude.

The crisis had been averted, but the experience had left an indelible mark on the team. They had faced a challenge, a threat to their collective well-being, and they had overcome it together.

They had learned the importance of teamwork, the value of diversity, and the power of collaboration. They had learned that even in the most chaotic of workplaces, a shared sense of purpose could bring people together, creating a sense of unity and strength that could withstand even the most difficult of challenges.

The office, once a collection of individuals, had become a team, a force to be reckoned with, united by their shared experiences and their unwavering commitment to making their workplace a better, more harmonious environment.

A Plan to Unite

The tension in the office was thicker than the stale coffee brewing in the communal pot. Every glance, every muttered word, every misplaced stapler felt like a potential detonator for a full-blown office war. The relentless schemes, intended to create order, had backfired spectacularly, leaving behind a trail of crumpled paperwork, shattered mugs, and bruised egos.

The office drama queen, known for her fondness for gossip and dramatic flair, had been demoted to the role of office pariah. Her carefully curated network of whispers and rumors had been exposed, leaving her with a reputation more tattered than the company's budget spreadsheets. The procrastinator, once a master of last-minute miracles, now found himself drowning in a sea of unfinished tasks and missed deadlines. His once-celebrated ability to thrive under pressure now felt like a curse.

Amidst the chaos, a glimmer of hope emerged. The collective realization that their individual efforts to tame the office beast had only made it wilder prompted a desperate search for a unified approach. The colleagues, bruised but not broken, gathered in a huddle, the scent of desperation mingling with the faint aroma of stale pizza from last night's failed attempt at a team-building pizza party.

"Look," said Sarah, the normally reserved marketing manager, her voice surprisingly firm, "we're all going down in flames if we keep fighting each other. We need to find a common goal, something we can all rally around."

The room fell silent. The weight of their collective failures hung heavy in the air. They all knew Sarah was right. The office had devolved into a battlefield, and they were all casualties.

"What about the company picnic?" suggested Mark, the sales manager, his voice tinged with uncertainty. "We've always had one, and everyone loves the free food."

A wave of groans swept through the room. The company picnic, a yearly tradition that was supposed to be a time for camaraderie and good food, had become a casualty of the office chaos. The previous year's picnic, a disastrous affair marked by spilled drinks, lost children, and a misplaced pie-eating contest trophy, was a testament to the office's dysfunctional state.

"No, no, no," said David, the resident data analyst, who had been eerily quiet throughout the debacle. "The picnic is too… superficial. We need something with more substance, something that reflects the real issues."

David's words were like a splash of cold water in the face. The room shifted, a collective sigh escaping their lips. David was known for his logic and analytical approach, and his words carried a certain weight.

"What do you suggest then?" asked Sarah, her eyes reflecting a flicker of hope.

"We need to fix the root of the problem," David declared, his voice gaining confidence. "The root of our chaos lies in our inability to communicate and work together effectively."

"So, what's your plan?" asked Mark, his skepticism evident.

"A team-building exercise, but not your average office picnic," David replied, a mischievous glint in his eye. "Something that will force us to collaborate, to build trust, and to see each other as colleagues rather than adversaries."

The colleagues exchanged glances, a mixture of curiosity and cautious optimism in their eyes. The prospect of a non-traditional team-building exercise held a certain appeal. They had tried everything else, from motivational posters to office zen gardens, with limited success. Perhaps, they thought, this could be their chance to finally turn the tide.

"Okay, we're listening," said Sarah, her voice betraying a hint of excitement.

David's plan, though unorthodox, was surprisingly compelling. He proposed a series of challenges that would require each of them to rely on their strengths and support each other's weaknesses. He suggested a series of "escape room" scenarios, each designed to test their communication, problem-solving, and critical thinking skills.

"Escape rooms?" questioned Mark, his eyebrow raised in skepticism. "Are we really going to waste our time playing games?"

"These aren't just games, Mark," David retorted, his voice firm. "These are strategic exercises designed to simulate real-world situations. We'll be facing challenges that require us to think outside the box, to work collaboratively, and to leverage our unique skills."

The idea took root in the minds of the weary colleagues. It offered a glimmer of hope in a world where their desks seemed to be sinking into a sea of despair. They weren't sure if it would work, but they were willing to give it a try. The prospect of escaping the office labyrinth of chaos and frustration was more appealing than staring down yet another mountain of unfinished tasks.

"So, you're saying we're going to be solving riddles and finding clues?" asked Susan, the perpetually cheerful administrative assistant, her voice filled with a mixture of trepidation and enthusiasm.

"Exactly," replied David, his eyes sparkling with a newfound zeal. "We'll have to work together to decipher codes, solve puzzles, and ultimately, escape the room. It's a test of our collective intelligence and teamwork."

The office, which had been filled with an atmosphere of silent despair, started to hum with a new kind of energy. The colleagues, finally united by a shared goal, felt a surge of hope. They were ready to step outside their comfort zones, to embrace the challenge, and to escape the wreckage of their chaotic work lives.

The escape rooms were not your typical "find the key and open the door" scenarios. David had meticulously crafted each challenge to reflect their unique work-related challenges and the personalities of the team. There was the "budget-balancing puzzle," where they had to allocate resources and make tough choices to avoid going bankrupt. There was the "data analysis enigma," where they had to decipher complex charts and graphs to unravel a hidden clue. There was the "communication conundrum," where they had to navigate a series of intricate messages to solve a puzzle.

Each challenge was a journey through their shared frustration, their individual quirks, and their collective ability to overcome adversity. They discovered that the procrastinator's ability to work under pressure was essential in finding solutions under time constraints. The office drama queen's keen eye for detail proved invaluable in deciphering subtle clues. Even the once-misunderstood data analyst's logic and problem-solving skills became crucial in navigating the complexities of the escape rooms.

As they worked together, the colleagues began to see each other in a new light. They discovered hidden talents and unexpected strengths. The office drama queen, stripped of her gossipy façade, became a valuable asset, her keen observation skills coming to the fore. The procrastinator, forced to contribute, surprised everyone with his quick thinking and creative solutions. The data analyst, initially perceived as aloof and detached, emerged as a leader, his logical approach bringing order to the chaos.

The escape room experience, initially perceived as a desperate attempt to escape their chaotic work environment, became a catalyst for a much-needed transformation. It forced them to confront their own behaviors, to recognize the strengths of their colleagues, and to embrace a new approach to collaboration.

The office was still far from perfect. There were still moments of frustration, misplaced paperwork, and the occasional burst of office drama. However, the escape room experience had ignited a spark of unity, a shared understanding that their collective well-being depended on their ability to work together.

As they stepped out of the final escape room, victorious and exhausted, a sense of shared accomplishment filled the air. They had conquered not only the puzzles but also their own biases and limitations. The office had become a place where collaboration was not just a word, but a lived reality. They had, in their own quirky way, escaped the wreckage of their dysfunctional work environment, emerging stronger and more unified than ever before.

The Great CleanUp

The air in the office crackled with a strange mix of energy: excitement, anxiety, and a faint whiff of desperation. It was the day of the Great Clean-Up, a monumental effort to tame the beast of disorganization that had been plaguing their workplace for far too long. The mastermind behind this daring endeavor was none other than Martha, the office's self-proclaimed "organizational guru." Her enthusiasm, though bordering on maniacal, was infectious, and for once, even the most resistant colleagues found themselves swept up in the tide of change.

The scene was a sight to behold. Stacks of overflowing file cabinets stood like towering monuments to procrastination, their contents a mishmash of crumpled papers, forgotten reports, and half-eaten lunches. Desk drawers resembled bottomless pits, where lost pens and forgotten projects lay buried beneath layers of dust and despair. The coffee machine, an epicenter of office life, was a sticky battleground, where remnants of past spills and forgotten mugs clung to its metal surface.

The first step was to conquer the paper mountains, and the colleagues, armed with paper shredders, recycling bins, and an arsenal of brightly colored folders, descended upon the chaos with a vengeance. The air was thick with the sound of paper ripping, staplers clicking, and the occasional sigh of frustration. The aroma of coffee, strangely enough, seemed to blend harmoniously with the smell of stale paper and cleaning supplies.

It was a scene worthy of a post-apocalyptic movie, except instead of zombies, they were battling the remnants of a paper-based civilization. And in the midst of the mayhem, humor emerged like a beacon of hope. A misplaced stapler became a source of playful banter. A crumpled memo, its message indecipherable, inspired a round of impromptu poetry. The seemingly endless task of sorting through mountains of paper became a shared experience, binding them together with laughter and a shared sense of purpose.

The procrastinator, Harold, who was usually found hiding behind a fortress of crumpled papers, seemed to experience a strange metamorphosis. He found himself surprisingly motivated, fueled by a newfound sense of responsibility and perhaps a touch of guilt. His desk, once a chaotic landscape of overflowing coffee cups and forgotten snacks, slowly transformed into a haven of neatness and order.

As the hours ticked by, the office began to resemble a construction zone. Dust swirled in the air, fluorescent lights cast long shadows, and the sound of boxes being moved echoed through the halls. The coffee pot brewed tirelessly, providing a steady flow of caffeine to keep them fueled through the grueling task.

Despite the progress, there were moments of despair. The office drama queen, Barbara, who was notorious for her gossip-fueled dramas, stumbled upon a particularly juicy piece of information hidden within a pile of discarded emails. Her eyes widened with a mix of excitement and fear. This discovery threatened to derail the entire clean-up effort, sending the office back to its chaotic roots.

The colleagues, however, had learned to work together, their camaraderie forged in the fires of office chaos. They knew that if they wanted to reclaim their sanity, they had to confront this new threat head-on. They devised a plan, a cunning strategy to neutralize Barbara's gossip before it could spread like wildfire.

The plan, while audacious, was surprisingly effective. Barbara, caught in the crossfire of their ingenious scheme, found herself unexpectedly isolated. Her gossip, once a source of power and intrigue, had become a liability, her carefully constructed narratives falling apart under the weight of their collective scrutiny.

The Great Clean-Up, though initially fueled by desperation, had ignited a spark of hope within the office. It was a testament to the power of collaboration, a reminder that even the most messy situations can be resolved with a touch of humor, a dash of ingenuity, and a whole lot of teamwork. The office was far from perfect, but it was a place where colleagues had learned to work together, to laugh together, and to find a semblance of order amidst the chaos. The Great Clean-Up was not just a cleaning spree; it was a transformative experience, a journey that had brought them closer together and, dare they say, a little less messy.

Obstacles and Opportunities

The air crackled with anticipation as the office embarked on the grand clean-up. It was a moment of truth, a reckoning for their chaotic ways. Each desk, each corner, each forgotten file held a testament to their collective disarray. But amidst the clutter, a sense of purpose emerged. The team, united in their desire for order, was ready to tackle this monumental undertaking.

Initially, the clean-up resembled a frenzied dance of misplaced enthusiasm. Papers flew, folders tumbled, and the air filled with the sound of frantic shuffling. The meticulous planner, Amelia, felt a pang of frustration as she watched the disorganized pile up in the corners, their efforts seeming to create more chaos than they eradicated.

However, amidst the initial disarray, opportunities began to sprout. The procrastinator, Michael, discovered a hidden talent for sorting through the mountain of emails. Instead of his usual last-minute panic, he found a surprising sense of accomplishment in tackling the daunting task. This unexpected surge of motivation was a revelation, even to him. The office drama queen, Stephanie, found a newfound purpose in organizing the overflowing supply closet. As she meticulously sorted through the forgotten office supplies, Stephanie realized that even chaos could be tamed with a little bit of focus.

The clean-up, far from being a tedious chore, became a shared adventure. Laughter erupted from the cubicles as the team stumbled upon long-forgotten treasures – a moldy box of expired cookies, a forgotten rubber chicken, and a collection of oddly-shaped paperclips. Each discovery, however absurd, provided a moment of shared laughter and relief, helping to lighten the mood and foster a sense of camaraderie. Humor became the glue that held them together, bridging the divides of their messy past.

The process of restoring order unearthed a hidden trove of creativity. Amelia, ever the pragmatist, discovered a knack for designing an innovative filing system. Michael, inspired by his newfound efficiency, drafted a comprehensive guide for managing email clutter. Stephanie, embracing her newfound orderliness, created a beautiful visual representation of their team's progress.

The clean-up wasn't just about physical organization; it was about a shift in mindset. It was about letting go of old habits and embracing new ways of working. It was about recognizing the value of collaboration, the power of laughter, and the potential for growth that existed within their seemingly chaotic world.

As the team emerged from the dust cloud of the clean-up, a sense of accomplishment settled over them. The office, though still a far cry from pristine, was now a space that felt hopeful, optimistic. The air, once thick with the scent of coffee and stale pizza, now had a faint whiff of freshly-cleaned surfaces and fresh beginnings.

But even in the face of their newfound order, a sense of trepidation lingered. The journey to a truly organized office was a long one, with unforeseen challenges still lurking around every corner. They had learned that even the most organized plans could unravel, that even the most determined individuals could succumb to the lure of chaos. They had also learned that within their messy world, they had found a strength they never knew they possessed.

The clean-up was just the first step, a stepping stone to a brighter future. But for now, they relished the newfound sense of order, the camaraderie forged in the crucible of chaos, and the faint promise of a future where their collective work lives were less about wreckage and more about synergy. The battle for order was far from over, but they were armed with a newfound sense of hope and humor, ready to face whatever chaos lay ahead.

The Procrastinators Redemption

The Great Clean-Up was a sight to behold. It was like a scene out of a post-apocalyptic movie, but instead of zombies, there were piles of paperwork, overflowing recycling bins, and a crusty coffee pot that seemed to have a life of its own. The office, once a haven of organized chaos, had transformed into a battlefield of clutter.

Amidst the pandemonium, a surprising figure emerged. It was our very own procrastinator, who, until recently, had been notorious for his ability to conjure deadlines out of thin air. His office, a shrine to disorganization, had become a monument to his chaotic work style. But today, a glimmer of something different shone in his eyes.

"Okay, folks," he declared, a newfound sense of purpose radiating from his usually laid-back persona, "Let's get this show on the road! We have a mountain of paperwork to conquer, a sea of misplaced files to navigate, and a coffee pot to exorcise its demons!"

The office erupted in a mix of laughter and surprised murmurs. The procrastinator, who had previously been the champion of procrastination, was now leading the charge towards order. His transformation was as shocking as it was unexpected.

"I've had a revelation," he confessed, a hint of shame creeping into his voice, "This whole mess...it's getting out of control. My own office looks like a hurricane hit it, and I've been contributing to the problem more than anyone else."

A wave of sympathy swept through the office. Even the office gossip queen, who usually reveled in the chaos, felt a flicker of admiration for the procrastinator's honesty.

"So, I'm putting my foot down," he continued, his voice gaining confidence with each word, "No more last-minute rushes, no more drowning in paperwork, no more pretending I can control the chaos. It's time for a change, and I'm leading the way!"

His words resonated with the other office members. The stress of the overwhelming mess had been weighing on everyone, and seeing the procrastinator take the initiative to change sparked a sense of hope.

"We're in this together," he declared, his eyes gleaming with a newfound sense of responsibility, "And together, we can turn this mess into something manageable. We can create a haven of organization and sanity, where deadlines are met, files are found, and the coffee machine behaves like a civilized citizen!"

His words ignited a spark of camaraderie within the office. The colleagues, who had previously bickered and blamed each other for the chaos, found themselves united in their shared desire for a more organized workplace.

The Great Clean-Up, initially driven by a sense of desperation, now transformed into a shared mission. The procrastinator, once the embodiment of chaos, was now the unlikely leader of this new order. His conversion to the cause of organization was a testament to the power of self-reflection and the surprising depths of even the most disorganized soul.

The office buzzed with activity. Files were sorted, emails were answered, and desks were cleared. The procrastinator, now the "Procrastinator Emeritus," as someone jokingly dubbed him, even ventured into the realm of time management, offering advice on prioritizing tasks and setting realistic deadlines.

"Look, I may not be an expert on time management," he confessed, a sheepish smile on his face, "But I've certainly mastered the art of procrastination, and I can tell you from experience that it's not a winning strategy. It just creates more stress and chaos."

His newfound insights surprised everyone. It was as if the procrastinator had undergone a metamorphosis, shedding his old chaotic skin to reveal a more organized and responsible individual underneath.

As the day wore on, the office began to take shape. The piles of paperwork dwindled, the recycling bins were emptied, and the once-dreaded coffee machine even seemed to be producing decent coffee.

The office, once a haven for chaos, was starting to resemble a place where work could actually get done. And at the heart of this transformation stood the procrastinator, the unlikely hero of organization.

"You know," the office gossip queen remarked, her voice laced with surprise and admiration, "I never thought I'd see the day when the procrastinator would become the champion of order. Maybe there's hope for us all after all."

The procrastinator, who had once been the embodiment of procrastination, smiled. It was a genuine smile, one that reflected a sense of accomplishment and a newfound sense of purpose.

"We've come a long way," he admitted, "But it wasn't about me. It was about us. We all had a part to play in this mess, and now we're all working together to clean it up."

The Great Clean-Up was a success. The office, though still far from perfect, was a testament to the power of collective effort and the surprising resilience of the human spirit. The procrastinator, the office gossip queen, and all their colleagues had learned valuable lessons about the importance of order, the power of teamwork, and the unexpected hero that can rise from the depths of procrastination.

As the last of the files were filed, the procrastinator stood back and surveyed the office. It was no longer a haven for chaos, but a space where work could be done, where ideas could flourish, and where, most importantly, a team could come together to face the challenges ahead. And at the center of it all, the procrastinator, once the champion of disorganization, was now the unlikely hero of organization, a testament to the power of self-reflection, the importance of teamwork, and the transformative potential of a good dose of humor in the face of chaos.

Humor as a Tool

The office was buzzing with a chaotic energy, like a hive of bees that had accidentally stumbled into a sugar factory. It was a scene of utter disarray, a symphony of unorganized chaos, a visual representation of the term "organized mess." Amidst this whirlwind of paperclips, sticky notes, and forgotten lunchboxes, the team had decided it was time to take matters into their own hands. They knew that, in this office, chaos was the norm, and that meant they had to take charge, wrangle the wreckage, and reclaim their sanity.

The first step was to face the beast that was the procrastinator, a creature who thrived on the adrenaline rush of eleventh-hour deadlines. He was a master of weaving narratives of impending doom, a dramatic flair that would make Shakespeare jealous. He was like a runaway train, with a cargo hold full of unfinished tasks, hurtling towards a cliff of catastrophic deadlines.

"We need to find a way to reel him in," one colleague whispered, "to help him understand that the world won't end if he starts a project a day or two before it's due."

"He needs a reality check," another colleague added, "a healthy dose of structure to help him see the light at the end of the tunnel."

The team's plan was as ambitious as it was audacious: they decided to introduce the procrastinator to the concept of "time management." The problem was that they had to do it without breaking his spirit or, heaven forbid, making him even more frantic. It was a tightrope walk with a potential for a spectacular, and very public, fall.

The team decided to use a subtle approach, strategically placing Post-it notes around his workspace, each one containing a simple, non-threatening reminder: "Start now," "Break it down," "Time is ticking," "Don't panic." It was a visual language of encouragement, urging him to embrace the discipline of a schedule.

The results were... mixed.

The procrastinator, who was used to functioning on the brink of disaster, found the reminders a bit too much. He found himself staring at the brightly colored squares, wondering if they were meant for him. He was sure they were, but he refused to acknowledge the fact. The team, however, decided to double down, adding even more sticky notes. They felt like they were on the verge of a breakthrough, that their efforts were finally starting to pay off.

But as the week progressed, the office became a battleground of Post-it notes. They were everywhere, a chaotic collage of color and urgency. Some were strategically placed on his computer screen, some attached to his coffee mug, others even tucked into his pockets. It was a well-intentioned, but ultimately misguided, effort.

As the procrastinator found himself surrounded by a sea of Post-it notes, he began to unravel. His once-casual demeanor morphed into a simmering panic. He was overwhelmed by the sheer number of reminders, his mind racing with anxieties he hadn't felt before. His desk was a whirlwind of scattered papers, sticky notes, and a growing sense of dread.

The office, in the meantime, became a playground for the Post-it note army. It was like a chaotic game of tag, with each employee adding their own messages to the mix, their enthusiasm overshadowing the fact that the procrastinator was slowly spiraling out of control.

In the midst of this sticky note chaos, the team was beginning to realize their mistake. Their well-intentioned efforts to help were inadvertently causing more harm than good. The office was becoming a colorful disaster, and the procrastinator, overwhelmed, was beginning to look like he might just implode.

As they surveyed the scene, one of the colleagues, who had a knack for seeing the silver lining in any situation, offered a solution. "I think," he said, with a mischievous twinkle in his eye, "we need to introduce humor into the equation."

"Humor?" another colleague responded, "How could humor help?"

The colleague chuckled. "It's simple," he explained, "we can use humor to diffuse the tension and build camaraderie. Think about it, when we laugh, we feel less stressed. And when we feel less stressed, we're more likely to work together effectively."

The team, still slightly wary of their previous endeavors, was cautiously optimistic. "But how do we introduce humor without making the situation worse?" one colleague asked.

"We can start by adding a little bit of playful banter to the office," the colleague responded, "and maybe throw in some lighthearted jokes."

The plan was simple: inject humor into the office environment, with the goal of making the work experience more enjoyable and, in the process, easing the tension that had taken root. They started with a few harmless pranks:

placing a rubber chicken on the procrastinator's chair, replacing his coffee with a cup of decaffeinated, and changing his phone background to a picture of a sloth.

The office, once a battlefield of sticky notes, started to transform. Laughter replaced frantic whispers, and the team, united in their shared sense of amusement, began to approach the situation with a newfound perspective.

The procrastinator, who had initially been flustered by the antics, was now a willing participant. The rubber chicken, he decided, was actually a good luck charm, and the sloth on his phone became a symbol of his newfound embrace of slow and steady work habits. The decaf coffee, however, was a different story.

The team's journey was far from over. They were still navigating the murky waters of office chaos, but their approach had shifted. Instead of trying to force order upon a team that was resistant to it, they learned to use humor as a tool to build camaraderie and ease the tension. The office was still a bit messy, a bit chaotic, but it was a more enjoyable, a more lighthearted, and a more productive space. And the team, united by their shared sense of humor and their determination to overcome the wreckage, was ready to face whatever challenges came their way, one rubber chicken, one sloth, and one decaffeinated cup of coffee at a time.

A Glimpse of Harmony

The office had a strange, almost electric energy buzzing through it. It wasn't the usual caffeine-fueled jitters, but something subtler, a hopeful anticipation. The Great Clean-Up, as they'd dubbed it, was finally underway. It started with a hesitant push, a reluctant sigh, and a few murmured complaints about "who left this mess here?" But then, as if a switch had flipped, a collective wave of energy swept through the office.

The chronic procrastinator, Mr. Last-Minute himself, had surprisingly taken the lead. He'd been a master of distraction, of turning deadlines into thrilling narratives of near-misses, but now, he was organizing stacks of paperwork with surprising enthusiasm. Maybe it was the newfound sense of control, or maybe it was the fact that a colleague had threatened to "borrow" his beloved coffee mug if he didn't pull his weight. Whatever the reason, he was suddenly the picture of efficiency.

The office drama queen, who normally thrived on chaos, found herself surprisingly quiet. The whispers and gossip had been replaced by the gentle hum of the vacuum cleaner and the satisfying click of folders being sorted. She even offered to brew a pot of coffee, much to everyone's surprise. It seemed that even the most dramatic personalities could find a sense of purpose in the face of a shared goal.

The humor that had been used to mask the tension was now a tool for building camaraderie. Jokes were cracked, stories were shared, and laughter echoed through the office as they worked. There was a newfound lightness in the air, a sense of shared accomplishment that transcended the messy paperwork and overflowing bins.

As the day wore on, the office was slowly but surely transforming. Stacks of paper dwindled, desks were cleared, and the once-unfamiliar scent of coffee replaced the lingering aroma of stale pizza and forgotten lunches. The cluttered conference room, once a breeding ground for meetings that went nowhere, was now a space for collaboration and brainstorming. The office had become a place where people could actually work, where creativity could flourish, and where laughter was the soundtrack to their day.

The change wasn't instantaneous, of course. It was like watching a stubborn weed slowly giving way to a delicate flower. There were moments of frustration, of setbacks, and of course, the occasional outburst of "Why does this always happen to us?" But there was also a growing sense of optimism, a belief that they were actually making progress, that they could create a workspace that was as efficient as it was welcoming.

There were still challenges, of course. The office was like a ship that had been through a storm, with its deck littered with debris. But the storm had passed, and the crew was now working together to clear the wreckage, to repair the damage, and to prepare the ship for smoother sailing ahead.

There was a sense of camaraderie, a shared purpose, a realization that they were all in this together. The office had been a battlefield of personalities, a warzone of misplaced files and forgotten deadlines. But now, the battle lines were blurred, and the focus was on a common goal.

The office wasn't perfect, not by a long shot. There were still moments of frustration, and the occasional sigh of resignation. But there was also a newfound respect, a recognition that they could achieve more together than they could ever achieve alone. The chaotic symphony of disarray was slowly giving way to a harmonious melody of collaboration.

The office was a microcosm of the world, a place where personalities clashed and compromises were made. It was a place where dreams were dreamt, ambitions were fueled, and failures were learned from. It was a place where, despite the chaos, there was always the potential for something beautiful to emerge.

And in that moment, as the office hummed with the energy of shared effort, a faint flicker of hope ignited in the hearts of the employees. Perhaps, just perhaps, they could actually turn the chaos into something manageable, something sustainable, something even joyful. The battle for order wasn't over, but the battle was being won, one small step at a time.

In the coming days, there would be more challenges, more unexpected turns, more moments of frustration. But the office, once a battlefield of personalities, was now a place where the seeds of change had been planted. And as the dust settled, and the wreckage was cleared, a new sense of order, and a new sense of possibility, emerged.

A New Challenge Emerges

Just when the office was starting to resemble a somewhat organized and functional space, the universe, in its infinite amusement, decided to throw a wrench into the gears. It began subtly, with a faint tremor in the air, like the rumble of a distant earthquake. Then, the tremors escalated into a full-blown seismic shift, leaving the office in a state of utter disarray.

The culprit? A seemingly harmless email, sent out by the company's CEO, announcing an upcoming "Office Innovation Challenge." While the intention was to encourage creativity and collaboration, the announcement set off a chain reaction of unexpected consequences.

The challenge, a simple request to brainstorm ideas for improving workplace efficiency, ignited a fierce battle for dominance. The normally quiet and reserved office was suddenly transformed into a battleground of competing ideas and clashing egos. The air buzzed with nervous energy as everyone scrambled to outshine the others with their ingenious solutions.

But the challenge wasn't about finding the best solution, it was about proving who was the most clever, the most insightful, the most… well, everything. The office, which had recently tasted a sliver of peace, was now engulfed in a tempest of competitiveness.

The office drama queen, once a source of chaos and gossip, transformed into a ruthless strategist, her mind churning with schemes to sabotage her rivals. Her office walls were plastered with mind maps, each line and arrow representing a carefully constructed plan to discredit her colleagues and secure her own victory.

The procrastinator, once a master of last-minute miracles, found himself overwhelmed by the challenge. Instead of brainstorming ideas, he spent his days daydreaming about beach vacations, convinced that the whole ordeal was a conspiracy against his right to idle time.

The normally well-organized and efficient team leader, who had championed the office clean-up effort, was now caught in a whirlwind of conflicting opinions and clashing personalities. His carefully crafted plans for maintaining order were tossed aside as the office descended into a maelstrom of chaos.

The office's quietest member, known for their meticulous attention to detail and their unwavering ability to remain calm under pressure, emerged as a surprising leader. They saw through the office's power struggles and recognized that the true challenge wasn't about individual glory but about finding a solution that benefited everyone.

They organized a series of brainstorming sessions, creating a safe space for colleagues to share their ideas without fear of judgment or competition. They encouraged everyone to focus on the big picture, reminding them that the ultimate goal was to make the office a better place to work, not to win a personal battle.

The office's resident comedian, who usually found humor in the most stressful situations, struggled to find the funny side of this particular mess. The competition had brought out the worst in everyone, turning their usual lighthearted banter into barbed insults and thinly veiled sarcasm.

But even in the midst of the chaos, a glimmer of hope emerged. The office's shared experience of the challenge, despite all the stress and tension, brought them closer together. They began to see each other not as rivals, but as teammates, united by a common goal.

The office's resident cynic, who had long been skeptical of the team's ability to change their ways, was surprised to find himself drawn into the collaborative spirit. He began to see the value in working together, realizing that even in the face of adversity, they were stronger as a team.

The unexpected challenge had thrown the office into a whirlwind of chaos, testing their unity and revealing their true characters. But as they navigated this new terrain, they began to discover a deeper understanding of themselves and each other. The challenge, while initially unwelcome, had become a catalyst for growth and change. It had forced them to confront their weaknesses, learn from their mistakes, and embrace the importance of teamwork.

The office was still a far cry from perfectly organized, but there was a newfound sense of purpose, a shared understanding that they were in this together, and that, despite the occasional bumps in the road, they would find a way to make it work. The office, once a breeding ground for chaos and conflict, had become a laboratory of resilience, where laughter, collaboration, and a little bit of humor would help them navigate the inevitable challenges ahead.

The Reckoning

The office was a battlefield, a warzone of misplaced documents, forgotten deadlines, and a constant symphony of clattering keyboards and frustrated sighs. The air crackled with a palpable tension, a silent acknowledgment of the storm brewing beneath the surface. The culprit? A seemingly innocuous email, a simple request for a project update. It was the catalyst, the match that ignited the tinderbox of pent-up frustration and resentment that had been simmering for weeks.

The email was addressed to everyone on the team, a casual reminder that a looming deadline was rapidly approaching. It was a gentle nudge, meant to encourage a bit of urgency. But for the team, already teetering on the edge of chaos, it felt like a declaration of war. The procrastinator, our resident master of the last-minute scramble, saw it as an opportunity to revel in the adrenaline rush of working under pressure. The office drama queen, always eager to stir the pot of office gossip, interpreted it as a chance to dissect the sender's motives and find fault.

The atmosphere was thick with the scent of impending doom, a sense that the calm before the storm was about to break. The colleagues, once united by a shared sense of frustration, were now divided by their differing interpretations of the email. Some were simply resigned to the inevitability of chaos, others were actively fueling the flames, and a few brave souls were desperately trying to hold onto a sliver of sanity.

The chaos had become a vicious cycle, an ever-spinning carousel of missed deadlines, half-finished projects, and a

constant state of confusion. The office had become a
breeding ground for stress, a breeding ground for
resentment, and a breeding ground for laughter. Yes,
laughter. For amidst the chaos, a strange sense of humor
began to emerge. The colleagues, united by their shared
misery, found a strange comfort in the absurdity of their
situation. They joked about the impossible deadlines, they
shared stories of their failed attempts at organization, and
they laughed at their own misfortune.

The first scheme to tame the chaos was a masterpiece of
logistical brilliance. The team, united in their desire for
order, decided to implement a system of color-coded folders,
a meticulous schedule for project meetings, and a daily
check-in to ensure everyone was on the same page. It was a
bold attempt, a brave leap into the unknown.

But the unforeseen consequences were as predictable as a
thunderstorm in monsoon season. The color-coded folders,
designed to bring clarity and order, became a battlefield for
territorial battles. The procrastinator, known for his penchant
for leaving things until the last minute, saw the folders as an
opportunity to unleash his artistic side. He would adorn them
with whimsical doodles, a misplaced doodle that led to a
mix-up of crucial documents.

The drama queen, always eager for a bit of intrigue, began
using the folders as a platform for her subtle gossip
campaign. A stray comment scrawled on a sticky note, a
cleverly placed photo, and the office was buzzing with
speculation. The email system, meant to improve
communication, became a breeding ground for
misunderstandings. The procrastinator, his inbox bursting
with unread emails, would send out a hasty reply, often
forgetting to attach the necessary documents.

The schedule for project meetings, meant to streamline communication, became a source of frustration. The procrastinator, always running behind, would miss his assigned slot, leaving the meeting participants to wait for his arrival, a wait that often stretched into hours.

The check-ins, designed to monitor progress and ensure accountability, became an exercise in futility. The procrastinator, always a master of distraction, would cleverly spin tales of insurmountable obstacles, always finding a way to deflect blame. The drama queen would use the check-ins as a platform to air her grievances, transforming what was supposed to be a quick update into a rambling saga of workplace drama.

The office, once a haven of productivity, was now a swirling vortex of confusion and chaos. The schemes, initially conceived as a solution, had become a part of the problem. The colleagues, once united in their quest for order, were now fractured and demoralized. The humor, which had once offered a glimmer of hope, had grown stale, replaced by a dull ache of despair.

The office, once a haven of productivity, was now a swirling vortex of confusion and chaos. The schemes, initially conceived as a solution, had become a part of the problem. The colleagues, once united in their quest for order, were now fractured and demoralized. The humor, which had once offered a glimmer of hope, had grown stale, replaced by a dull ache of despair.

The tension in the air was thick enough to cut with a butter knife, a palpable sense of frustration and despair. The office, once a haven of productivity, was now a battleground for a new war, a war for sanity and a war for survival. The consequences of their actions, the repercussions of their failed schemes, were now looming over them like a storm cloud, threatening to unleash a torrent of chaos.

The first casualty of this war was the drama queen, the gossip-mongering architect of office intrigue. Her carefully crafted web of whispers and speculation began to unravel, revealing the cracks in her carefully constructed façade. Her carefully crafted story, a tale of victimhood and betrayal, was met with a wave of skepticism, a questioning of her motives and a realization that her carefully constructed persona was nothing more than a cleverly constructed facade.

Her downfall was swift and brutal, a swift execution by the very colleagues she had tried to manipulate. The truth, as it often does, had a way of revealing itself, a truth that exposed the cracks in her carefully constructed facade.

Her attempts to deflect blame, to spin tales of victimhood, were met with a collective sigh of resignation. The colleagues, weary of her constant drama, had finally reached their breaking point.

And so, the drama queen, the instigator of office chaos, found herself isolated, her attempts to manipulate and control the office environment met with a wall of indifference. The office, freed from her corrosive influence, began to heal, the wounds of her gossip slowly beginning to mend.

The consequences of their actions, the repercussions of their failed schemes, were now looming over them like a storm cloud, threatening to unleash a torrent of chaos. The office, once a haven of productivity, was now a battleground for a new war, a war for sanity and a war for survival.

And as the storm clouds gathered, the colleagues, once divided by their differences, found themselves united by a common goal - to weather the storm and emerge from the wreckage.

Unity Tested

The office, once a breeding ground for chaos, was finally starting to feel like a place where people could breathe. The "Great Clean-Up," fueled by the unexpected motivation of the procrastinator, had managed to wrangle the wreckage into some semblance of order. Even the drama queen, stripped of her gossip-fueled power, seemed to be embracing a new, less-dramatic persona. There was a strange sense of harmony in the air, a newfound respect for each other's quirks and a shared understanding that, despite the office's inherent messiness, they were all in this together.

But, as with any good fairy tale, this period of peace was destined to be disrupted.

It began with a seemingly harmless email, a notification about an upcoming company-wide competition. The prize? A trip to a tropical paradise for the entire office, a dream vacation that had the potential to bring even the most jaded employees out of their slumps. It was the kind of incentive that had the power to reignite the competitive spirit, to stir up the office drama that everyone thought they had finally left behind.

The competition was simple: the team with the most innovative and successful project would win. This, in itself, wasn't a problem. The problem was the team dynamic.

The office was still reeling from the fallout of the earlier schemes, the trust issues, the bruised egos. The once-united colleagues were now divided into factions, each with their own agenda. The procrastinator, finally embracing responsibility, was determined to lead a team and prove their worth. The drama queen, seeking redemption, was eager to contribute and show everyone she could be a valuable asset.

But the old habits, those ingrained patterns of behavior that had led to the office's initial chaos, were hard to shake.

The procrastinator, fueled by a newfound passion for the project, became obsessed with perfection. They spent countless hours on presentations, meticulously crafting every slide, driving their team members to the brink of exhaustion. Their meticulousness was commendable, but their fear of failure and need for absolute control began to stifle creativity.

The drama queen, seeking to prove her worth, started whispering in the ears of other teams, spreading rumors and undermining the progress of her own colleagues. This, of course, backfired spectacularly, leading to a barrage of accusations and mistrust.

The office, once a place of camaraderie, was becoming a battlefield. The unity forged through the earlier struggles was rapidly dissolving. The dream vacation, which had promised joy and relaxation, now loomed like a distant, unattainable goal.

The tension reached a breaking point during a team meeting. The procrastinator, fuelled by a blend of passion and anxiety, delivered a passionate presentation that was met with silence. The team, exhausted from the grueling hours and frustrated by the constant pressure, didn't respond. The drama queen, in a desperate attempt to regain control, whispered some unfounded gossip about a rival team, hoping to sow seeds of discord.

But the office, having learned from their past mistakes, was not swayed.

The team, led by a quiet but determined colleague who had always been overlooked, stood their ground. They politely but firmly addressed the procrastinator's concerns about perfection, reminding them that the competition was about innovation, not just presentation. They also confronted the drama queen, calling her out on her manipulative behavior and reminding her that their success would only come from working together, not against each other.

The room fell silent, the weight of the moment hanging in the air. The procrastinator, humbled by the team's response, realized they had become too focused on perfection and had forgotten the importance of collaboration. The drama queen, realizing that her actions had only served to harm the team, felt a wave of shame. The team, finally united in a common goal, decided to put their differences aside and focus on what they could accomplish together.

The office, once a place of disarray, was starting to find its rhythm. The procrastinator, while still prone to procrastination, embraced the team's guidance and learned to delegate tasks, allowing their creativity to flourish. The drama queen, humbled by her own actions, became a vocal advocate for collaboration, her gossip replaced with valuable contributions.

The trip to paradise, once a dream, was now a shared goal, a symbol of their resilience and teamwork. The office had faced its toughest challenge yet and, against all odds, they were coming out stronger. The chaos that had once threatened to derail them had become a catalyst for growth, a reminder that even in the most chaotic of environments, unity and collaboration could prevail.

The Drama Queens Redemption

The office buzzed with a tension thicker than the stale coffee brewing in the kitchenette. The air crackled with the unspoken fallout from the recent chaos. It was as though a storm had swept through the workplace, leaving behind a trail of lingering anxieties and fractured relationships.

The unexpected twist, a disastrous product launch gone awry, had thrown the office into a tailspin. The blame game had begun, pointing fingers at the procrastinator, the gossiping drama queen, and even the usually unflappable office manager. The unity forged in the wake of the initial clean-up efforts seemed to crumble under the weight of disappointment and the pressure to find a scapegoat.

Amelia, the self-proclaimed drama queen, found herself at the center of the maelstrom. Her penchant for spreading gossip, a habit she justified as "keeping everyone informed," had reached a fever pitch. A carelessly whispered comment, a seemingly harmless snippet of office gossip, had morphed into a rumor that threatened to derail the entire company.

Amelia, usually so adept at stirring the pot of office drama, now felt the heat of the flame she'd ignited. The whispers followed her like a shadow, and the pointed stares made her skin crawl. Her usual confidence, a shield built upon a foundation of rumors and innuendo, began to crack.

The weight of her actions, the damage her words had caused, began to sink in. She realized with a pang of guilt that her self-proclaimed role as the office gossip had gone too far. The gossiping, which had once felt like a harmless pastime, now felt like a weapon she'd wielded carelessly, leaving a trail of destruction in its wake.

In the aftermath of the product launch disaster, Amelia found herself ostracized. The office, once a stage for her daily dramas, now felt like a cold, desolate space. She retreated to her cubicle, a solitary island in a sea of disapproval.

As she sat, staring at the blank screen of her computer, a wave of self-pity washed over her. She felt trapped, suffocated by the silence of her colleagues, their muted whispers about her "reckless behavior." The blame for the product launch failure, amplified by the gossiping she'd spread, weighed heavily on her.

Suddenly, a gentle knock at her cubicle door startled her. It was Sarah, the office manager, a woman who'd always seemed impervious to Amelia's attempts to stir the pot. Sarah, with her calm demeanor and her knack for managing chaos, was the last person Amelia expected to see at this moment.

"Amelia," Sarah said, her voice soft and measured, "I wanted to talk to you."

Amelia, surprised by the unexpected visit, could only manage a hesitant nod.

"I know you've been going through a rough time," Sarah continued, "and I understand you're feeling overwhelmed by the situation. But I also know you're a good person, Amelia, and you're capable of much more than gossiping."

Sarah's words, spoken with a sincerity that touched Amelia's heart, broke through the wall of guilt and shame Amelia had built around herself.

"I'm sorry," Amelia whispered, tears pricking her eyes. "I made a mistake, and I didn't mean to cause so much trouble."

"I know you didn't," Sarah replied gently, placing a hand on Amelia's shoulder. "But we all make mistakes. It's what we do after those mistakes that matters. You have a chance to redeem yourself, Amelia, and I believe you can do it."

Sarah's words, like a balm to Amelia's wounded soul, gave her a glimmer of hope. The prospect of redemption, a path to rebuild her reputation and regain the trust she had so carelessly lost, felt like a lifeline.

Sarah went on to explain that the product launch failure wasn't solely Amelia's fault. The team had collectively missed vital checkpoints, and the gossiping, while damaging, was only one factor in a series of missteps.

Sarah's perspective, a breath of fresh air in the storm of guilt Amelia had been living in, opened her eyes to the broader context. She realized that while she had a part to play in the disaster, she wasn't solely responsible. This realization, coupled with Sarah's encouragement, ignited a spark of determination in Amelia.

She resolved to dedicate herself to repairing the damage she had caused. She promised to be a force for good in the office, a source of positivity and support, rather than the queen of office gossip.

The path to redemption, Amelia realized, wouldn't be easy. It would require honesty, humility, and a willingness to rebuild trust. But she was ready for the challenge.

Amelia started by reaching out to her colleagues, apologizing for her actions and expressing her commitment to change. Her apologies, sincere and heartfelt, surprised her colleagues, who had come to expect her to defend her gossiping habits.

But Amelia was determined to be better. She offered to help with the product relaunch, volunteering her skills in marketing and communication. She took the time to listen to her colleagues' concerns, offering words of encouragement and support.

As she worked side-by-side with her colleagues, Amelia found a sense of belonging she hadn't experienced before. She discovered the power of teamwork, the strength of shared purpose, and the joy of working towards a common goal.

Slowly but surely, Amelia's reputation began to shift. The whispers turned into murmurs of appreciation, the pointed stares softened into smiles. The office, once a stage for her dramas, transformed into a space of collaboration and camaraderie.

The drama queen, once a figure of gossip and intrigue, was now a force for good, a beacon of hope in the wake of the product launch disaster. Her redemption, a testament to the power of genuine change, reminded everyone that even in the most chaotic of situations, redemption is always possible.

Rising to the Occasion

The air in the office was thick with tension, a palpable energy that hummed beneath the surface of forced normalcy. The recent office-wide clean-up had seemed to work, for a while at least. The piles of paper were smaller, the desks were somewhat less cluttered, and the aroma of stale coffee had, for a few precious days, been replaced with the faint scent of air freshener. It was as if a fragile truce had been established, a temporary ceasefire in the ongoing war against disorganization.

Then, the unexpected happened. A rogue email landed in the inbox of the office manager, a chain of correspondence that was about to unravel everything they had painstakingly built. It was a message from a client, a high-profile account that held significant weight within the company. The subject line read: "Urgent: Project Delay."

A collective gasp rippled through the office as everyone, even the usually unflappable office manager, realized the gravity of the situation. The client's deadline had been pushed back, and the reason was a string of miscommunications and missed deadlines. It was, of course, all very confusing, a tangled web of misinterpretations and misplaced files.

"It's like a bureaucratic black hole," whispered Millie, the office assistant, a woman who could track down a misplaced paperclip with uncanny precision.

"It's like a tornado swept through our inbox," added Bob, the meticulous but perpetually overwhelmed accountant.

The office manager, a woman named Sarah who prided herself on her calm demeanor, found herself scrambling to make sense of the chaos. It was a classic case of "telephone tag," where information had been relayed from person to person, each time getting progressively more distorted.

"This is a disaster!" cried out Jessica, the office gossip queen, who, despite her penchant for spreading rumors, was surprisingly adept at keeping her own files organized.

"We can't afford a client like this to walk away!" added Mark, the ambitious sales manager, who always seemed to be on the verge of a panic attack.

The office was buzzing with panic. It was as if a switch had been flipped, sending them back to the days when their desks resembled miniature war zones and the email inbox was an unending labyrinth of urgent requests and missed deadlines.

Sarah, trying to remain calm, called an impromptu meeting. Everyone crowded into the tiny conference room, their faces grim as they stared at Sarah, waiting for her to deliver a solution. The air was thick with the unspoken anxieties of a team that knew they were on the brink of disaster.

"Listen, everyone," Sarah began, her voice unwavering despite the rising tide of fear. "We're in a bit of a pickle, but we've been through worse. We need to work together, pool our resources, and get this sorted out. There's no room for finger-pointing, blame, or the usual office drama. This is about all of us."

Her words echoed in the room, hanging in the air like a lifeline. It was as if a wave of shared responsibility had washed over them, erasing the internal walls that had been erected, the invisible boundaries that separated them.

"Remember the office clean-up?" Mark asked, his eyes widening with a new awareness. "It was chaos then, too, but we figured it out."

"And we were laughing about it too," added Millie, a faint smile playing on her lips.

The meeting was no longer a tense standoff; it was a moment of shared understanding. The realization that they were all in this together, that their individual contributions were essential to the team's success, hung in the air. The chaotic energy of the office had shifted, replaced by a newfound sense of unity.

"Okay, here's what we're going to do," Sarah announced, her voice now infused with newfound confidence. "We're going to divide and conquer. We're going to retrace the steps, starting with the initial client contact, and figure out exactly where things went wrong. And then, we're going to fix it."

The task was monumental, requiring every member of the team to work together. It was like a giant puzzle, each piece representing a different task, a different responsibility. The procrastinator, who was usually a source of stress, unexpectedly found himself contributing by meticulously reviewing each email, his meticulous nature a valuable asset in this time of crisis. The gossip queen, usually known for her penchant for spreading rumors, surprised everyone by taking charge of the internal communications, ensuring that everyone was on the same page and working towards the same goal. The sales manager, who was usually quick to panic, calmed down and focused on strategizing, leveraging his expertise in client relations to navigate the delicate situation.

Each individual brought their own unique skills and perspectives to the table, their differences becoming strengths rather than weaknesses. The office hummed with activity, a constant stream of emails, phone calls, and whispers as they worked tirelessly to solve the puzzle.

The atmosphere in the office was one of focused energy. A newfound sense of camaraderie replaced the usual office tension. There were moments of laughter, moments of frustration, moments of doubt, but through it all, they kept working together, a team united by a common goal.

As the sun began to set, casting long shadows across the office, they finally had a solution. It wasn't perfect, but it was a solution, a way to salvage the project and appease the client. Exhausted but exhilarated, they gathered around the office manager's desk, a sense of accomplishment filling the room.

"We did it," whispered Millie, her eyes shining with pride. "We actually did it."

"We did," Sarah confirmed, her voice thick with emotion. "We faced a new challenge, and we rose to the occasion. We're a team, and we're not afraid to work together."

As they all celebrated their victory, a quiet understanding settled over the office. They had learned a valuable lesson that day. Sometimes, the most unexpected challenges can bring people closer together, forcing them to see past their differences and embrace their shared goals. They had wrestled with the wreckage, and they had emerged stronger, a team ready to face whatever came their way.

Reevaluating Priorities

The office hummed with a newfound energy, a stark contrast to the frantic chaos that had once reigned supreme. The air was filled with a lighthearted buzz, a sense of accomplishment settling over the team like a warm blanket. Coffee mugs clinked together in celebratory toasts, laughter echoing through the hallways, a far cry from the tense silence that had once shrouded their shared space. It was as if the office had undergone a complete metamorphosis, shedding its chaotic skin to reveal a vibrant, cohesive unit, united by a shared sense of purpose.

The transformation hadn't been easy. There were moments of doubt, frustration, and a healthy dose of bickering, but through it all, they had learned to navigate their differences and work together to create a more harmonious environment. The procrastinator, once the embodiment of last-minute mayhem, had found a newfound sense of responsibility, his deadlines no longer looming over him like a storm cloud. The office drama queen, once a whirlwind of gossip and whispers, had discovered a new appreciation for constructive conversations and positive energy.

It was a revelation, a collective epiphany that changed everything. They realized that the path to a thriving workspace wasn't paved with elaborate schemes and forced order, but with a deeper understanding of themselves and their colleagues. They had learned to appreciate the unique quirks and strengths that each individual brought to the table, realizing that their differences, far from being weaknesses, were the source of their collective strength.

One afternoon, as the team gathered around the office coffee machine, sharing stories and laughter, a quiet reflection swept through the room. They had come a long way. They had weathered the storms of chaos, faced their own weaknesses, and discovered the power of true collaboration. They had learned that laughter, in its most genuine form, could be a potent antidote to stress and a powerful tool for building connections. They had discovered that, even in the most chaotic of environments, a shared sense of purpose and a commitment to each other could pave the way for a truly satisfying and fulfilling work experience.

Their journey had been fraught with challenges, but each hurdle they cleared solidified their bond, deepening their understanding of each other and their unique roles within the team. It wasn't about conforming to a cookie-cutter model of productivity; it was about embracing their individuality and finding a way to harmonize their strengths. It was a testament to the human spirit's ability to adapt, evolve, and ultimately, triumph over even the most daunting obstacles.

This new perspective shifted their focus from individual agendas to a collective vision. They started to see their work as a shared pursuit, a collaborative effort fueled by mutual respect and a genuine desire to succeed together. They were no longer a collection of individuals vying for recognition; they were a team, united by a common goal and a commitment to create something truly remarkable.

This shift in perspective wasn't just about work; it permeated their personal lives. They began to approach their relationships with a newfound sense of empathy, recognizing the power of collaboration and understanding. They were no longer just colleagues; they were friends, confidants, and allies, bound by their shared journey and the knowledge that they had overcome the chaos together.

The office, once a battlefield of conflicting personalities and chaotic work habits, had transformed into a haven of creativity, collaboration, and genuine connection. The walls, once adorned with crumpled papers and half-finished projects, now reflected the team's shared vision and the collective efforts that brought it to life. It was a tangible reminder of their journey, a testament to the power of self-reflection, empathy, and the indomitable spirit of teamwork.

They had discovered that the key to a thriving workplace wasn't about eliminating chaos entirely, but about finding a way to embrace it, to navigate it, and to ultimately turn it into an opportunity for growth and connection. They had learned to laugh in the face of adversity, to support each other through challenges, and to find joy in the journey, knowing that, together, they could achieve anything they set their minds to.

Their journey had been a testament to the power of transformation, reminding them that even in the most chaotic of environments, a shared vision and a commitment to each other could lead to a truly fulfilling and rewarding work experience. The office was no longer just a place where they earned a living; it had become a space where they thrived, where they learned, where they laughed, and where they discovered the true power of human connection.

As they continued their journey, they knew that the future held new challenges and unforeseen opportunities. But with the lessons learned, the bonds forged, and the spirit of collaboration burning brightly, they were ready to tackle whatever came their way. They were a team, a force to be reckoned with, ready to wrangle the wreckage, one laugh, one challenge, one shared accomplishment at a time.

Lessons Learned

The office hummed with a newfound energy, a stark contrast to the cacophony of chaos that had once reigned supreme. It was as if a giant, invisible hand had swept through the space, clearing the clutter of crumpled papers, half-eaten lunches, and abandoned coffee cups. The air itself felt lighter, infused with a shared sense of accomplishment.

As I settled into my desk, the quiet hum of the office felt almost surreal. It was a far cry from the days when the air crackled with tension, punctuated by the shrill ring of the phone and the incessant tapping of the drama queen's keyboard, composing another juicy gossip email. Now, the only sound was the gentle whirring of the air conditioner, a soundtrack to our collective relief.

This serenity was hard-earned, a testament to the rollercoaster ride we'd all been through. We'd started our journey as a motley crew of dysfunctional individuals, united only by our shared frustration with the office's chronic lack of order. The procrastinator, bless his heart, had a talent for transforming even the simplest task into a monumental endeavor, his desk a chaotic landscape of half-written reports, forgotten notes, and empty coffee mugs. The drama queen, with her penchant for whispered conversations and strategically placed sighs, was a walking, talking hurricane of office gossip, leaving a trail of anxiety and suspicion in her wake.

Our first attempt to tame the chaos had been an elaborate scheme, fueled by equal parts desperation and misplaced optimism. We'd naively believed that a system of color-coded folders and meticulously crafted schedules would magically transform our messy little world into a picture of efficiency. Instead, our well-intentioned efforts backfired spectacularly, leading to a chain reaction of misunderstandings and miscommunications.

As the dust settled from that initial debacle, we found ourselves questioning our approach. Maybe we were fighting the wrong battle. Perhaps the chaos wasn't an enemy to be conquered but a symptom of a deeper issue. We had to acknowledge that we weren't just dealing with a disorganized office; we were dealing with a group of disorganized individuals, each carrying their own baggage of quirks and habits.

We realized that we needed to embrace the individual, not just the chaos. We started by focusing on communication, fostering open dialogues about our struggles and insecurities. The procrastinator, when confronted with the reality of his procrastination, confessed that his fear of failure was paralyzing, leading him to delay tasks until the last minute. The drama queen, her mask of confidence shattered, admitted that she craved attention and validation, seeking solace in the shared drama that she fueled.

Slowly but surely, we began to understand each other, recognizing that beneath the surface of our seemingly chaotic behaviors lay a shared desire for connection and belonging. The office, once a battlefield of passive-aggressive emails and hushed whispers, transformed into a space of mutual respect and understanding.

Our shared journey through the chaos had taught us valuable lessons about ourselves and each other. We discovered that we were all capable of growth and change, that even the most deeply ingrained habits could be addressed with a little bit of introspection and a whole lot of empathy.

The office, once a symbol of disarray, now felt like a safe haven, a place where we could be ourselves, flaws and all, and still be embraced as a part of the team. The camaraderie we forged through our shared struggle had forged a bond stronger than any system or process. It was a reminder that even in the face of chaos, we could find hope, resilience, and a little bit of humor.

The Power of Teamwork

The office, once a battlefield of crumpled papers, forgotten deadlines, and whispered gossip, had undergone a metamorphosis. The air, once thick with tension and the scent of stale coffee, now hummed with a newfound energy, a vibrancy fueled by collaboration and a shared sense of purpose. The transformation was nothing short of remarkable.

The catalyst for this shift was, ironically, the very chaos that had threatened to engulf them. As colleagues united to wrangle the wreckage of their own disorganization, they discovered a hidden strength within themselves – the power of teamwork. It wasn't just about getting the job done; it was about recognizing that they were all in this together.

The once-reclusive procrastinator, whose penchant for eleventh-hour heroism had become legendary, discovered the joy of preemptive action. His newfound ability to anticipate deadlines and organize tasks surprised even him, fueled by the camaraderie of his colleagues. The office drama queen, who had once thrived on the whispers and murmurs of gossip, realized that her energy could be channeled towards something more constructive. She became a tireless advocate for team spirit, her gossiping instincts morphing into a knack for recognizing individual strengths and celebrating each other's successes.

The shared responsibility for the office's well-being sparked a sense of belonging, a feeling that their individual contributions were valued and celebrated. They learned to lean on each other's strengths, filling in gaps and providing support when needed. This newfound unity wasn't about erasing their individual quirks; it was about appreciating the diversity that made them unique and, ultimately, stronger.

Their journey wasn't without its bumps, of course. There were still moments of frustration, disagreements, and those inevitable moments of chaos that seemed to creep in like a persistent shadow. But now, they had a shared vocabulary for navigating these challenges, a common understanding that humor, even in the face of adversity, was their secret weapon.

Their shared laughter became a beacon, a reminder that they were in this together, and that even the most difficult situations could be overcome with a dose of humor and a good dose of team spirit.

This shift in perspective, the recognition that they were stronger as a team than they ever were individually, had a profound impact on their work. Their productivity soared, their ideas sparked, and their creativity bloomed. They were no longer a collection of individuals, but a cohesive unit, a team whose collective energy was unstoppable.

The office wasn't just a place to work; it was a space where friendships bloomed, where empathy flourished, and where laughter was the soundtrack to their shared journey. They had learned to embrace their differences, to recognize that their individual strengths, combined with their shared commitment to collaboration, could overcome any obstacle.

The transformation was visible in every corner of the office. Meetings, once dreaded sessions of tension and passive-aggressive glares, became brainstorming sessions filled with laughter and creative solutions. The once-cluttered break room, a testament to their collective forgetfulness, was now a haven of shared meals, spontaneous conversations, and the comforting aroma of freshly brewed coffee.

The change was not just about the physical space; it was about the shift in attitude, the realization that they were more than just colleagues; they were a team. This wasn't just a temporary fix; it was a fundamental change in their way of working, a new normal fueled by the power of teamwork, and seasoned with the magic of shared laughter.

Their journey from chaos to collaboration was a testament to the power of human connection, the realization that even the most dysfunctional of groups could find common ground and forge a path towards success. The office, once a haven of discord and disorganization, had become a sanctuary of collaboration, a place where individuals could flourish, and where teamwork became the foundation of a shared success story.

They had learned that while individual talent was important, it was the synergy of those talents, the commitment to support each other, the willingness to embrace their differences, and the shared belief in their collective strength that allowed them to wrangle the wreckage and create something truly remarkable. The office had become a microcosm of the world they wanted to see, a reflection of the power of teamwork, and a reminder that even in the most chaotic of environments, a shared sense of purpose could blossom. And as they navigated the future together, they knew that their shared laughter, a testament to their resilience and unity, would always be their guiding light.

Finding Common Ground

It wasn't as if they had planned to become best friends. In fact, most of them would have happily avoided each other if given the chance. But, as fate would have it, the office, like a melting pot of eccentric personalities, had thrown them together, their lives intertwined by the chaotic tapestry of shared spreadsheets, caffeine-fueled all-nighters, and those infamous office birthday cakes that seemed to always be a little... too enthusiastically decorated.

What began as a series of meticulously orchestrated schemes to wrangle the office's chaotic energy into a semblance of order had taken a surprising turn. The sheer volume of mishaps, near-misses, and accidental collaborations had inadvertently forged an unlikely bond between them. They had learned to laugh at the absurdity of their situations, to recognize the strengths that lay hidden within each other's idiosyncrasies, and to appreciate the camaraderie that bloomed amidst the chaos.

As the dust settled after their recent near-meltdown, they found themselves gathering around the office coffee machine, a ritual that had become less about the caffeine and more about the shared stories, the unspoken understanding. The procrastinator, once a champion of last-minute heroics, had found a newfound appreciation for deadlines, a quiet revelation born out of a series of well-intentioned but disastrously timed "urgent" projects. The office drama queen, her gossip well documented and her schemes thwarted, had discovered a peculiar sense of peace, a quiet satisfaction in contributing to the team's success instead of stirring the pot of office intrigue.

Their journey toward a more harmonious workplace wasn't without its bumps. They were still prone to the occasional eruption of frustration, the occasional burst of misplaced energy that sent a stack of folders tumbling toward the floor. But, they were also learning to manage their expectations, to anticipate the inevitable chaos that seemed to follow them like a shadow.

One afternoon, while huddled around the communal whiteboard, they were brainstorming ideas for their upcoming client presentation. The procrastinator, his usual sense of urgency replaced by a newfound sense of responsibility, offered up an innovative solution, a daring proposal that defied their usual conventions. The drama queen, her gossipy tendencies now channeled into a surprisingly effective marketing strategy, suggested a twist that added a touch of intrigue to the presentation.

The office had always been a place where ideas were thrown around like confetti, but this time, they felt a different energy. The ideas, once scattered and chaotic, were now coalescing, forming a cohesive vision that held the promise of a successful project. It was a vision that was born out of their collective efforts, a testament to the surprising power of unity that they had discovered amidst the wreckage of their chaotic past.

As they discussed their new vision, laughter filled the room, a spontaneous eruption of joy that reflected their newfound sense of belonging. The laughter was a testament to their ability to see the humor in their shared experiences, to recognize that even the most chaotic situations held the potential for growth and connection.

Later, as the sun set on another day, they left the office, their steps a little lighter, their spirits a little brighter. They were a team, a little unconventional, a little messy, but ultimately, a team that had found a way to wrangle the wreckage of their shared experience into something beautiful, something that held the promise of a future that was brighter, bolder, and a whole lot more fun.

Their journey to a more harmonious workplace had been one of trials and tribulations, a testament to the enduring power of laughter and collaboration. They had discovered that the path to a more productive and enjoyable office experience wasn't about eliminating chaos, but about learning to embrace it, to navigate it with a sense of humor and a commitment to teamwork.

And so, their story unfolds, a tale of messy colleagues who, through the power of shared experiences, learned to embrace the chaos, to find common ground, and to create a workspace that was not only productive, but also, unexpectedly, filled with laughter, camaraderie, and the quiet satisfaction of knowing that they had weathered the storm together, one chaotic episode at a time.

A New Beginning

The air in the office felt different. Lighter. Brighter. It wasn't just the sunshine streaming through the windows, though that certainly added to the pleasant ambiance. No, the change was more profound, a shift in the very atmosphere, a tangible sense of optimism that permeated every corner of the room.

It was a stark contrast to the weeks prior, when the office had resembled a hurricane's aftermath, a cacophony of disarray and disgruntled employees. It had been a relentless battle against an insidious enemy: disorganization. The enemy had taken many forms – procrastination, gossip, endless email threads, and a pervasive sense of apathy that had threatened to consume the very essence of their once-harmonious workplace.

The turning point had been the infamous "Office Clean-Up" – a monumental effort that had resulted in more chaos than order, with piles of misplaced documents, shredded paper confetti, and a bewildered intern trapped in a filing cabinet. But amidst the absurdity, a spark of unity had ignited. They had laughed at the chaos, at their own clumsiness, and most importantly, at the sheer ridiculousness of their predicament.

The office's resident procrastinator, Harold, who had previously reveled in the mayhem, found himself unexpectedly motivated. Seeing his colleagues' genuine efforts to salvage the situation sparked a surprising sense of responsibility in him. He started arriving at the office earlier, actually completing tasks on time, and even volunteered to organize the office potluck, an event that had previously been a logistical nightmare.

The office drama queen, Brenda, was initially skeptical. She had thrived on the drama, the gossip, the constant stream of office gossip. But witnessing the team's newfound camaraderie left her feeling strangely… irrelevant. As the office transformed into a space of cooperation and shared laughter, Brenda felt an undeniable urge to contribute, to be a part of something positive for once.

The change wasn't immediate, nor was it perfect. The occasional misplaced document, the stray gossip, the email thread that went rogue, all served as reminders of their past struggles. But they were a testament to the office's progress. They were reminders that even in a chaotic workplace, humor, resilience, and a willingness to work together could pave the path to a brighter, more productive future.

The office became a microcosm of the world at large, a space where people with diverse personalities, quirks, and proclivities learned to coexist, even thrive. They were reminded that everyone had something valuable to contribute, that even the most chaotic situations could be turned around with a little bit of effort, a healthy dose of humor, and a willingness to forgive and forget.

One afternoon, as the office buzzed with activity, the team gathered around the newly organized office kitchen. The aroma of freshly brewed coffee hung in the air, a welcome change from the stale coffee that had become a symbol of their former despair. Harold, sporting a freshly ironed shirt, poured everyone a cup, a gesture that would have been unthinkable just a few weeks ago.

"To a new beginning," he declared, raising his mug. The team, with a mix of amusement and genuine gratitude, joined in, their clinking mugs echoing a sentiment that reverberated through the room. The air, once heavy with tension, now vibrated with optimism.

The transformation wasn't just about a cleaner office or a less-chaotic workflow. It was about a newfound sense of purpose, a shared commitment to something bigger than themselves. It was about embracing their flaws, acknowledging their mistakes, and learning to work together in a way that was both productive and satisfying.

They were no longer a collection of individuals struggling to survive the daily grind. They were a team, a band of colleagues united by a shared vision, a collective commitment to creating a workplace that was not only functional but also fulfilling.

The journey had been bumpy, filled with obstacles and detours. But they had emerged stronger, wiser, and with a newfound appreciation for the power of teamwork, the importance of communication, and the life-affirming magic of a good laugh.

They had learned that even in a world of office politics, gossip, and procrastination, a shared sense of purpose could transform a workplace into a space of camaraderie, creativity, and ultimately, shared success. They had learned that even in the face of chaos, they had the power to "wrangle the wreckage" and create something beautiful, something truly exceptional.

Changing Roles

The office had become a whirlwind of activity, a kaleidoscope of personalities vying for attention. It wasn't just about the work anymore; it was about the personalities, the quirks, the dramas. It was a constant battle to keep the peace, and sometimes, it felt like a losing battle.

The procrastinator, once a source of amusement, had become a symbol of frustration. His last-minute rushes were no longer funny, but rather a source of anxiety for his colleagues. His inability to manage his time had led to a domino effect of delays and missed deadlines, causing a ripple effect that echoed throughout the office.

The office drama queen, ever the purveyor of gossip and intrigue, found herself in a precarious position. Her constant whispering and rumor-mongering had alienated her colleagues, and her tendency to exaggerate situations had backfired spectacularly. Her attempts to manipulate events to her advantage often resulted in unforeseen consequences, leaving her scrambling to salvage her reputation.

The office gossip had become the target of their schemes, and this time, the plan was to expose her for the drama queen she truly was. They devised a plan to reveal her manipulations, a sort of "truth serum" that would cut through her carefully constructed facade.

Initially, the plan seemed foolproof. They'd use her own words against her, exposing her lies and manipulations. They imagined her unraveling under pressure, forced to admit her guilt and apologize for her actions. But things rarely go as planned in this office.

The first step in their plan involved gathering evidence. The team diligently collected snippets of gossip, recorded her whispered pronouncements, and documented her manipulative tactics. The evidence was convincing, but it was a double-edged sword. They realized that exposing her might not only be embarrassing but could also trigger a backlash.

The plan was implemented, the "truth serum" was administered. They waited with bated breath for her meltdown, ready to witness her downfall. But instead of confessing and apologizing, she doubled down.

Her eyes narrowed with defiance, her voice rising in indignation, she proclaimed her innocence. "I never said any of those things!" she exclaimed. "You're all just trying to discredit me, to make me look bad!"

This unexpected turn of events threw the entire office into disarray. The colleagues were caught off guard by her unyielding denial, and they found themselves facing the consequences of their own actions. Instead of exposing her as the drama queen they had intended, they had inadvertently turned her into a martyr.

The office became a battlefield of whispers and accusations. The drama queen, now a victim of their manipulation, was suddenly the most powerful person in the office. Her lies, once a source of amusement, were now seen as truths, and her words carried a weight they had never possessed before.

The colleagues found themselves struggling to regain control of the situation. Their carefully crafted plan had backfired spectacularly, leaving them in a more chaotic state than before. They had inadvertently created a monster, and now they were forced to deal with the consequences.

The once-peaceful office was now a war zone, a breeding ground for suspicion and distrust. The colleagues, once united in their desire for order, were now divided, pitted against each other by the drama queen's manipulations. The office was a wreck, and it was only getting worse.

The colleagues realized they had to come together and find a new strategy. They needed a plan that didn't rely on manipulation and deception. They needed to find a way to work together, to use their strengths to overcome the challenges they faced.

Their task was daunting, but they had to find a way to restore harmony to their chaotic workplace. It was time to put aside their differences and work together to reclaim the office, to "wrangle the wreckage" they had inadvertently created. The fate of the office, and their sanity, rested on their ability to find common ground and work together as a team.

The weight of their responsibility weighed heavily on their shoulders. They knew the path ahead would be challenging, but they had to try. They were the only ones who could save their office, and their sanity, from the wreckage they had created.

Building Bridges

The office hummed with a newfound energy, a far cry from the chaotic cacophony that had once defined its existence. The air, once thick with tension and the lingering scent of stale coffee and procrastination, now carried a refreshing breeze of collaboration and shared purpose. It was as if a collective sigh of relief had swept through the cubicles, replacing the constant hum of anxiety with a harmonious melody of progress.

This transformation wasn't a magical overnight miracle. It was the culmination of a series of trials, tribulations, and, most importantly, laughter. The team, once a disjointed collection of personalities clashing like tectonic plates, had gradually molded into a cohesive force, their individual quirks now playing a harmonious role in the office orchestra.

The chronic procrastinator, once a master of last-minute miracles and a notorious source of pre-deadline panic, had become the unexpected champion of creative problem-solving. Their ability to think outside the box, fueled by a potent blend of caffeine and adrenaline, had blossomed into a valuable asset. They had even started showing up to meetings a few minutes before the scheduled time, a testament to their newfound sense of responsibility.

The office drama queen, once a self-proclaimed expert in office gossip and the orchestrator of countless unnecessary conflicts, had found a new purpose in spreading positivity. Their innate charisma and knack for storytelling now served to uplift the team's spirits and foster a sense of camaraderie. They had even discovered a talent for baking and frequently surprised their colleagues with homemade treats, turning their gossip sessions into delightful afternoon tea parties.

The key to this metamorphosis, surprisingly, was humor. It had become the office's secret weapon, the mortar binding the bricks of their newfound unity. Even in the face of setbacks, the team found a way to laugh, turning their frustrations into shared jokes and inside anecdotes. It was a subtle shift in perspective, a recognition that even in the most challenging situations, a lighthearted approach could make all the difference.

The office, once a breeding ground for frustration and despair, was now a sanctuary of creativity and collaboration. It was a place where humor was not merely tolerated but celebrated, a place where differences were embraced and where the collective good outweighed individual anxieties. It was a testament to the power of human connection, the transformative potential of shared experiences, and the undeniable truth that even the most chaotic situations can be navigated with a healthy dose of laughter and a willingness to build bridges.

One afternoon, during a particularly challenging project, the team found themselves facing an unexpected roadblock. The deadline loomed, the pressure mounted, and the usual suspects—the procrastinator, the drama queen, and a handful of other characters whose names were whispered in hushed tones—began to sweat. The tension in the air was thick enough to slice with a butter knife.

But then, a miracle happened. Someone, no one is quite sure who, started cracking jokes. The office drama queen, ever the master of theatrics, launched into an impromptu stand-up routine, riffing on the absurdity of the situation. The procrastinator, ever the embodiment of spontaneous chaos, chimed in with a series of witty observations, turning their procrastination into a source of humor. The rest of the team, emboldened by their example, followed suit, their laughter echoing through the hallways, dispelling the cloud of negativity that had threatened to engulf them.

The tension dissipated, replaced by a shared sense of amusement. The seemingly insurmountable obstacle suddenly seemed less daunting. The team, united by laughter, found a creative solution, a testament to the power of humor to ignite ingenuity and overcome adversity.

As the weeks turned into months, the office transformation continued. The team, no longer bound by their individual quirks but empowered by their collective strength, tackled new challenges with renewed enthusiasm. They had learned that true success wasn't about eliminating chaos but about embracing it, transforming it into an opportunity for growth and shared joy.

The office, once a battleground of conflicting personalities, had become a vibrant tapestry of diverse talents woven together by the threads of laughter, collaboration, and a shared desire to make the most of the messy, unpredictable, and utterly fascinating experience that is office life.

But it wasn't all sunshine and rainbows. The office, like a well-oiled machine with a few loose screws, still had its moments of hiccups and mishaps. The procrastinator, despite their progress, would still occasionally vanish into the ether just days before a deadline, forcing the team to scramble to pick up the pieces. The office drama queen, although transformed into a beacon of positivity, would still occasionally revert back to their old ways, whispering gossip in the shadows.

But these moments, instead of being met with frustration and despair, were now treated as opportunities for growth and learning. The team, united by their shared experiences, had learned to embrace the imperfections, to find humor in the chaos, and to use these challenges as opportunities to strengthen their bonds and refine their teamwork.

The office, once a source of stress and anxiety, had become a place of laughter, camaraderie, and shared purpose. It was a testament to the power of human connection, the resilience of the human spirit, and the undeniable truth that even in the most chaotic situations, a little bit of humor can go a long way.

In the end, the office was no longer a collection of individuals trying to survive another day. It was a team, united by their shared journey and their unwavering belief in the transformative power of humor and collaboration. It was a testament to the fact that even the most disorganized group of people can find a way to "Wrangle the Wreckage" and emerge stronger, wiser, and most importantly, with a healthy dose of laughter along the way.

Creative Solutions

The office had undergone a transformation. Gone were the days of rampant chaos, replaced by a newfound sense of order and camaraderie. But as the dust settled, a few lingering problems remained, like a persistent itch that wouldn't quite go away. The procrastinator, while no longer a master of last-minute mayhem, still struggled with deadlines. The gossip queen, while humbled by her past mistakes, found it hard to resist a juicy piece of office gossip. And the once-infamous coffee machine, though now diligently cleaned, still occasionally malfunctioned, threatening to plunge the office back into caffeinated chaos.

The team, however, was undeterred. Having learned the hard way that a chaotic office was not a recipe for success, they embraced a new approach: **creative problem solving.** The procrastinator, recognizing his weakness, proposed a "pre-procrastination" strategy. He would tackle tasks in advance, breaking them down into smaller, more manageable steps, ensuring that deadlines were met without resorting to eleventh-hour panic attacks. The gossip queen, realizing the damage her whispers had wrought, decided to channel her energy into a positive direction. She established an "office positivity board," where colleagues could share encouraging notes and uplifting quotes, fostering a more positive and supportive work environment.

As for the troublesome coffee machine, the team decided to adopt a "coffee machine lottery." Each week, a different employee would be responsible for cleaning and maintaining the machine, ensuring its optimal performance. This not only kept the machine running smoothly but also fostered a sense of shared responsibility, reminding everyone that even the smallest task could have a significant impact.

But the office wasn't just about tackling problems; it was about building a workplace that fostered creativity and joy. The team introduced "creative brainstorming days," where colleagues could gather to brainstorm innovative ideas, share their thoughts freely, and encourage one another. These sessions were a testament to the power of collaboration, showcasing the diverse talents and perspectives within the team.

To encourage a sense of fun and camaraderie, they implemented a monthly "office game night." This provided a space for colleagues to unwind, bond over shared interests, and laugh together, reminding everyone that work shouldn't be all work and no play. These games, ranging from trivia nights to board games, provided an outlet for healthy competition while fostering a sense of team spirit.

The office had become a microcosm of creative problem solving, where challenges were met with innovative solutions and setbacks were turned into opportunities for growth. The team had discovered that humor was not just a way to survive the chaos; it was a powerful tool for building resilience, fostering camaraderie, and reminding everyone that even in the midst of work-related challenges, there was always room for laughter and joy.

This newfound sense of unity had a ripple effect, transforming the office into a space where colleagues felt valued, respected, and truly connected. They had learned that the key to a thriving workplace was not just about efficiency and productivity; it was about creating a space where individuals felt empowered to be their best selves, where humor and creativity were embraced, and where challenges were met with a collective spirit of collaboration.

But their journey wasn't over. There would be new challenges, unforeseen obstacles, and moments of frustration along the way. But now, armed with the lessons learned, the power of humor, and a renewed sense of team spirit, they were ready to tackle whatever came their way, knowing that together, they could wrangle the wreckage and create a workplace that was not only efficient but also enjoyable, rewarding, and truly their own.

The Humor Factor

The office was buzzing with a palpable energy, a strange mix of anxiety and amusement. It was like the atmosphere after a particularly raucous game of office charades – a sense of shared experience, a slight hangover of absurdity, and a lingering, unacknowledged tension.

This newfound energy wasn't born out of an inspirational team-building retreat or a sudden influx of lucrative contracts. No, this energy was the aftermath of their latest scheme – an attempt to wrangle the office's chaotic energy into a semblance of order. Their efforts, however, were about as effective as trying to organize a pack of squirrels on a sugar high.

The mastermind behind this "Operation Tidy Desk" was a meticulous spreadsheet guru named Agnes, a woman whose own workspace was a testament to her organizational skills. Agnes believed, with a fervor that bordered on religious conviction, that a tidy desk was a sign of a tidy mind, and a tidy mind was the key to productivity.

Unfortunately, their office wasn't exactly brimming with tidy minds. They had Penelope, the resident procrastinator, who thrived on the adrenaline rush of last-minute deadlines. Then there was Beatrice, the self-proclaimed office drama queen, whose gossip-fueled rants could rival a Shakespearean tragedy.

Agnes, however, was determined to bring order to this chaotic symphony of personalities. With a PowerPoint presentation that could rival a military strategy briefing, Agnes outlined her plan. The first step was a mandatory office-wide "Desk Clean-Up Day," an event so meticulously choreographed, it could have been mistaken for a corporate ballet.

However, their meticulously crafted plan was promptly derailed by a rogue stapler. It all started innocently enough. Penelope, while trying to avoid a crucial deadline, had accidentally tossed the stapler over her cubicle wall. It landed with a resounding thud, missing Agnes' meticulously organized pile of papers by a hair.

The stapler incident ignited a chain reaction of mishaps. Beatrice, who had been diligently working on her latest office gossip masterpiece, felt compelled to join in the chaos. She launched into a dramatic monologue about the stapler's "unfortunate demise," sending the office into a frenzy of nervous laughter.

And then, of course, there was the infamous incident of the runaway office coffee pot. Agnes, in a misguided attempt to bring a touch of calm to the chaos, had inadvertently left the coffee pot unattended. The result was a steaming, caffeinated tsunami that wreaked havoc on the office's delicate ecosystem.

But amidst the wreckage, a peculiar thing began to happen. The shared experience of navigating this hilarious, albeit disastrous, chaos seemed to create a bizarre camaraderie. It was like they were all in on a grand joke, a joke that only they, the inhabitants of this chaotic office, could truly appreciate.

Humor, it seemed, was the unexpected glue that held them together. It was their shared language, their coping mechanism, their secret weapon against the encroaching darkness of office disarray. It was a reminder that even in the face of the most absurd and chaotic situations, a little laughter could go a long way.

The "Desk Clean-Up Day" ended with a sense of accomplishment that was more about survival than actual tidiness. The office was still a bit of a mess, but it felt different. It felt like they had all weathered a storm together, and in the aftermath of the storm, a new kind of camaraderie was blossoming.

Their collective laughter was a testament to the fact that even amidst the chaos, they had found a way to find humor in the absurdity. And in the wake of their shared experience, the office wasn't just a place to work, it was a space where they could be themselves, flaws and all, and laugh together through the inevitable messiness.

A Sense of Belonging

The office, once a battlefield of misplaced deadlines and passive-aggressive post-it notes, was now a haven of unexpected camaraderie. The air buzzed with a newfound energy, a sense of purpose that had been missing for far too long. The colleagues who had once viewed each other with suspicion, even animosity, now saw each other as partners in a shared mission: to not only wrangle the wreckage of their messy work habits, but also to build a foundation for a more productive and fulfilling work environment.

It wasn't just a simple matter of ticking boxes on a to-do list or achieving a certain level of organization. It was about a transformation of mindset, a recognition that they were in this together. The chronic procrastinator, once infamous for his last-minute bursts of frantic activity, was now a champion of early deadlines, his newfound efficiency a source of quiet pride. The office drama queen, her gossip-fueled whispers now replaced with genuine interest in her colleagues' well-being, even found herself volunteering to organize team-building activities. The once-dreaded coffee breaks transformed into moments of genuine connection, laughter, and shared stories.

The sense of belonging was palpable, a tangible shift in the office's atmosphere. No longer was the office simply a place to clock in and clock out, a necessary evil to earn a paycheck. It had become a space for shared dreams, a platform for personal and professional growth. It was a place where individuals, once isolated by their own quirks and anxieties, found a sense of belonging, a space where their unique strengths could contribute to a collective good.

The transformation wasn't without its hiccups, of course.
There were still days when the old habits threatened to
resurface, when the stress of deadlines threatened to shatter
the newfound harmony. But the team had learned to weather
the storm, to laugh off the occasional misstep, to offer
support and encouragement instead of judgment and blame.
They had learned that embracing imperfections was not a
sign of weakness, but a necessary step in building a truly
cohesive unit.

The office, once a breeding ground for chaos, was now a
testament to the power of collaboration. It was a reminder
that even the most disorganised individuals, when united by
a common goal, could achieve remarkable things. The team
had not only wrangled the wreckage of their messy work
habits but also forged an unbreakable bond, a testament to
the human spirit's ability to rise above adversity and embrace
a sense of belonging.

The transformation was not only evident in the office's
outward appearance. It was reflected in the individuals
themselves. They were more confident, more engaged, and
more willing to take risks. They were no longer defined by
their weaknesses, but by their shared strengths. The office,
once a battleground for egos, was now a sanctuary for
collaboration, a testament to the human spirit's ability to find
common ground and create something beautiful from the
wreckage.

It was a transformation that extended beyond the office
walls, seeping into their personal lives. They were more
patient, more understanding, and more willing to
compromise. They were less afraid to ask for help, and more
willing to offer it. The lessons they had learned in the office,
in the crucible of shared chaos, had forged them into a
stronger, more resilient unit.

One Friday afternoon, as the team gathered for their weekly after-work drinks, a sense of accomplishment hung in the air. They had come a long way. They had wrangled the wreckage of their messy work habits, and in the process, they had discovered something far more precious - a sense of belonging. The office, once a source of stress and anxiety, was now a source of pride and purpose. It was a place where they could be themselves, where they could be heard, where they could contribute to something bigger than themselves.

The journey had been bumpy, but they had emerged stronger, more united, and more confident. They had learned that even in the most chaotic situations, humor and teamwork could prevail. They had learned that even the most disorganised individuals, when united by a common goal, could achieve remarkable things. And most importantly, they had learned that a sense of belonging could be the most powerful force for change. As they clinked their glasses in a toast to their shared journey, a wave of warm contentment washed over them. They were a team, a family, a band of misfits who had wrangled the wreckage of their lives, and in the process, discovered the true meaning of success - a shared sense of belonging, a shared purpose, and a shared laugh.

Settling into Routine

The office, once a breeding ground for chaos and procrastination, had undergone a remarkable transformation. It was as if a mystical force had descended, sweeping away the dust bunnies of disarray and ushering in an era of order and efficiency. The air itself felt lighter, the coffee machine hummed with newfound purpose, and the office gossip mill had been replaced by a symphony of productivity. It was a sight to behold.

The once-dreaded weekly meetings, previously marred by rambling tangents and impromptu sing-alongs, now flowed smoothly, punctuated only by the occasional "Amen" from the enthusiastic but easily distracted marketing guru, Brenda. Even the dreaded "Potluck Friday," where dishes ranging from lukewarm spaghetti to mysteriously gelatinous concoctions had once been the norm, now boasted an impressive array of culinary delights, thanks to the collaborative efforts of the entire team.

The notorious procrastinator, Harold, who had previously lived by the mantra, "Why do today what you can postpone until tomorrow?" had experienced a surprising epiphany. He discovered that completing tasks, no matter how mundane, could actually be… enjoyable? Shocking, I know. Apparently, the realization that his constant delays were not only creating unnecessary stress but also dragging down the entire team, finally dawned on him. And so, Harold, the previously notorious "last minute Larry," emerged as a champion of timeliness, much to the astonishment of his colleagues.

Meanwhile, the office drama queen, Veronica, had found a new outlet for her penchant for gossip. Instead of spreading rumors about colleagues' personal lives, she became an enthusiastic champion of positive news. She had taken to posting uplifting quotes on the office bulletin board, much to the amusement of her colleagues who had once considered her the office's resident "bad news bear." Now, her newsfeed consisted of inspirational messages like, "Be the change you wish to see in the world" and "You are capable of amazing things." The transformation was so profound that even Veronica's best friend, the office gossip enthusiast, had started questioning her sanity.

The office's new routine was far from perfect. There were still moments of chaos, like the day the office coffee machine decided to revolt, spewing forth a geyser of lukewarm coffee that drenched the office's most dedicated worker, the ever-efficient and perpetually impeccably-dressed accountant, Mr. Smith. But even then, the office responded with a collective shrug, a shared chuckle, and an immediate collective effort to clean up the mess.

This newfound harmony wasn't simply about the absence of chaos, it was about something deeper, something that transcended the mere fulfillment of tasks and deadlines. It was about camaraderie, respect, and the understanding that each individual was a valuable part of a larger whole. The office, once a battleground of personalities and conflicting work styles, had become a tapestry woven together by mutual respect and a shared commitment to success.

This transformation was not the result of a magical spell or a sudden influx of workplace zen gurus. It was the culmination of many small, seemingly insignificant acts of kindness, understanding, and a willingness to step outside of one's comfort zone. It was a reminder that even in the most chaotic of workplaces, a shared sense of purpose and a touch of humor can go a long way in fostering a positive and productive environment.

The office had become a testament to the power of positive change, a beacon of hope for those who believed that the workplace was destined to be a breeding ground for chaos. It proved that even the most dysfunctional of teams could transform into a cohesive unit, capable of achieving great things, as long as they were willing to embrace the power of collaboration, communication, and a healthy dose of laughter. And as the team celebrated another successful week with a celebratory pizza party (yes, even the office potlucks had become more… palatable), they all knew that their journey towards a more harmonious workplace had only just begun. They had learned that even in the most chaotic of environments, order could emerge, and that the office, once a battlefield, could become a haven of teamwork and camaraderie.

There were, of course, some lingering remnants of the office's former chaotic self. The occasional misplaced stapler, a forgotten lunchbox left in the communal fridge, and the persistent tendency of the office printer to jam at the most inopportune moments. But these were minor inconveniences, easily navigated by a team that had learned to embrace the unexpected with a smile and a shared chuckle.

The office had found its rhythm, its new normal. It was a symphony of productivity, punctuated by bursts of laughter, a testament to the power of shared experiences and the bonds that could be forged when colleagues learned to work together, embrace their differences, and navigate the messy world of office life with a healthy dose of humor. It was a reminder that even in the most chaotic of environments, a shared sense of purpose and a touch of humor could go a long way in fostering a positive and productive environment.

It was a beautiful thing, this new normal, this office transformed. It was a place where colleagues weren't just co-workers, they were a team, a family, united in their shared journey towards a better, more productive future.

And so, the office continued on, its new rhythm a testament to the power of collaboration, communication, and a healthy dose of humor. They had wrangled the wreckage, and in the process, they had discovered that even the most chaotic of workplaces could become a haven of teamwork and camaraderie. It was a journey that had begun with chaos and ended with a symphony of productivity, a story that would be told and retold, reminding future generations of office workers that even in the face of the most daunting of challenges, the power of teamwork, humor, and a shared sense of purpose could prevail.

Celebrating Successes

The office buzzed with a new energy, a tangible shift from the chaotic days of yore. The once-dreaded Monday morning meetings were now lively brainstorming sessions, fueled by coffee and camaraderie. Gone were the days of whispered complaints and passive-aggressive post-it notes; in their place bloomed a spirit of cooperation and mutual respect. The air, once thick with tension, now hummed with a newfound sense of purpose.

The transformation wasn't a sudden, dramatic shift, but rather a slow, steady evolution. It started with small, almost imperceptible changes, like a hesitant smile across the office, a shared laugh at a misplaced stapler, or the surprising absence of a gossip-fueled drama. These tiny victories, celebrated with genuine delight, solidified the fragile foundation of trust that had emerged from the ashes of chaos.

One afternoon, as the team celebrated a successful project launch with a collective sigh of relief, the office drama queen, once the queen of petty squabbles, surprised everyone with a heartfelt toast. "To the power of teamwork," she declared, raising her glass. "To the chaos that brought us together, and to the strength we found within each other." The room erupted in applause, a cacophony of cheers and clinking glasses, echoing the sentiment of a team finally finding its footing.

The once-procrastinator, now a champion of deadlines, proudly presented his meticulously organized spreadsheet, a testament to his newfound efficiency. His transformation, a source of amusement for his colleagues, was celebrated with genuine admiration and respect. They understood that the struggle to break old habits was real, and his dedication to change was a victory for everyone.

The office's success wasn't just about ticking boxes on a project list; it was about the evolution of the individuals within it. They had learned to recognize their strengths, celebrate their differences, and embrace the beauty of collaboration. They learned that even the most chaotic situations could be navigated with humor, empathy, and a willingness to work together.

This spirit of collaboration extended beyond the office walls, seeping into their personal lives. They found themselves organizing impromptu potlucks, volunteering for community events, and even forming a weekend hiking group. The camaraderie they had forged in the office had become a source of strength and support, a reminder that even in the face of life's unpredictable twists and turns, they could rely on each other.

The office, once a breeding ground for frustration and despair, had become a sanctuary of laughter, creativity, and mutual respect. They celebrated their victories, both big and small, with a newfound appreciation for the power of teamwork and the magic of human connection. The office's new normal was a testament to their resilience, their determination to overcome the chaos, and their unwavering belief in the power of collaboration.

The change was not without its challenges, of course. There were still moments of frustration, disagreements, and the occasional misplaced stapler. But now, instead of succumbing to negativity, they tackled these challenges head-on, their laughter echoing through the office as they navigated the inevitable bumps in the road.

They had learned that the journey from chaos to harmony
was not linear, but rather a winding path filled with
unexpected twists and turns. But with each step they took,
with each hurdle they overcame, their bond grew stronger,
their confidence soared, and their belief in the power of their
collective spirit solidified. They were a team, a family,
bound together by a shared experience, a shared journey, and
a shared vision for a better future. They had wrangled the
wreckage, transformed the chaos, and created a new normal,
a testament to the power of humor, teamwork, and the
human spirit's resilience.

Challenges Revisited

The office, once a chaotic whirlwind of procrastination and gossip, had finally found its rhythm. The air was lighter, the laughter more frequent, and the once-dreaded Monday mornings now felt like a chance to catch up with friends. It was a remarkable transformation, a testament to the resilience and humor of the office team.

They'd learned a lot about themselves and each other during the tumultuous journey, and the scars of past battles were now badges of honor. The procrastinator, who once reveled in last-minute deadlines, had discovered a newfound sense of purpose, finding satisfaction in completing tasks ahead of schedule. The office drama queen, once addicted to the thrill of gossip, had found her voice in constructive communication, channeling her energy into collaborative brainstorming sessions.

As they sat around the conference table, sharing a celebratory potluck (no one dared to suggest a theme this time), the team reminisced about the wild ride. The memories were still fresh, the laughter still echoed in the air.

"Remember that time we tried to create a 'productivity chart'?" chuckled Sarah, the quiet but observant marketing assistant, her voice tinged with amusement. "It ended up being a giant, colorful mess, with sticky notes clinging to every available surface."

"And the time we attempted a 'stress-free office initiative'?" added Ben, the ever-optimistic project manager, his eyes twinkling. "Turns out, giving everyone free bubble wrap didn't exactly inspire calm."

The laughter erupted again, a symphony of shared memories. They'd learned that even the most well-intentioned schemes could go hilariously wrong, that even in the face of absurdity, they could find humor and ultimately, a path to a more harmonious workspace.

They'd faced their fears, their weaknesses, and their own tendencies to succumb to chaos. They'd learned that even the most stubborn procrastinator could find motivation, that even the most dramatic gossip queen could discover the power of positive communication. And they'd learned that even in the midst of workplace mayhem, a dash of humor could be the key to unlock a newfound sense of camaraderie.

"Do you remember the 'coffee machine incident'?" asked Emily, the office's resident tech whiz, a mischievous grin spreading across her face. "When the machine decided to start brewing lukewarm coffee, and everyone went ballistic?"

The memory sparked a new round of laughter, a collective sigh of relief escaping their lips. It was a reminder that they'd come a long way, that they'd faced adversity, and that they'd emerged stronger, more united, and definitely more appreciative of a good cup of coffee.

As the potluck dwindled and the laughter subsided, the team settled into a comfortable silence. They all felt a deep sense of gratitude for this newfound harmony, for the bonds they had forged, for the journey they had shared.

The office wasn't perfect. There were still moments of tension, disagreements, and the occasional burst of spontaneous chaos. But now, with the lessons of the past etched in their minds, they had the tools to navigate the rough waters, to celebrate the victories, and to embrace the messy, humorous beauty of their shared experience.

"We're like a dysfunctional family, but somehow, it works," said Mark, the quiet and introverted designer, his voice soft but sincere.

The others nodded in agreement, a silent understanding passing between them. They were a team, a family, a group of individuals brought together by circumstance and united by their shared desire to wrangle the wreckage and create a workplace that felt more like a haven than a battlefield.

They had embraced the chaos, learned from their mistakes, and found humor in the unexpected. And in doing so, they had transformed a chaotic office into a place where laughter, collaboration, and genuine connection reigned supreme. The office wasn't perfect, but it was theirs, a space they had built together, brick by brick, with a healthy dose of laughter and a whole lot of heart.

And they knew, as they looked at each other, a shared sense of satisfaction glowing in their eyes, that this was only the beginning. The office, once a scene of workplace havoc, was now a testament to the power of resilience, the magic of humor, and the strength of a team united by a shared journey.

The Art of Compromise

The office had become a delicate ecosystem, a fragile balance of personalities and quirks, each contributing to the overall harmony—or lack thereof—of the workplace. After the initial chaos of the "Great Clean-Up" and the subsequent wave of unforeseen challenges, a new rhythm had emerged. The office hummed with a newfound sense of camaraderie, the air buzzing with a mix of laughter and focused productivity. There was a sense of shared accomplishment, a collective understanding that they had weathered the storm together, emerging stronger on the other side.

But even in this newfound tranquility, the ever-present threat of chaos lurked around every corner. It was like trying to maintain a spotless white tablecloth at a picnic in a windy field; a single sneeze could send crumbs flying, threatening to undo the meticulous efforts of tidying up. Maintaining this newfound order required constant vigilance, a delicate dance of compromise and communication, and a healthy dose of humor to navigate the inevitable bumps along the way.

The art of compromise had become a crucial skill in this newly evolved office dynamic. The procrastinator, once a master of the last-minute rush, had embraced a more structured approach, though his tendency to leave things until the eleventh hour still occasionally caused a ripple of anxiety. The office drama queen, with her insatiable appetite for gossip, had found a new outlet for her energy— organizing office events, where her sharp wit and penchant for drama were channeled into creating memorable occasions.

The colleagues who had once clashed over the placement of the office coffee machine or the temperature of the thermostat had found a way to coexist, respecting each other's quirks and preferences. It wasn't a perfect harmony, but it was a marked improvement from the chaotic free-for-all that had defined their days before.

The power of compromise extended beyond the individual personalities. The office had developed a system of checks and balances, a shared understanding of how to navigate the inevitable conflicts and disagreements that arose. They had learned to see each other's perspectives, to appreciate the strengths and weaknesses that made up their team. And they had learned to laugh at their mistakes, to find humor in the inevitable chaos that life, and office life in particular, inevitably threw their way.

It wasn't always easy. There were days when the old habits threatened to resurface, when the pressure of deadlines or the lure of office gossip threatened to pull them back into the familiar chaos. But they had a new weapon in their arsenal: a shared sense of purpose, a belief that they could create a better work environment together.

One of the most significant changes was the shift in their approach to problem-solving. They had learned that the most effective solutions were not those imposed from the top down, but those that emerged through collaboration and compromise. They had learned that the best ideas came not from individuals working in isolation, but from a team that shared ideas, perspectives, and experiences.

The art of compromise, it turned out, was more than just a skill; it was a philosophy. It was the understanding that no one had all the answers, that even the most well-intentioned plans could backfire, that flexibility and a willingness to adapt were essential to navigating the ever-changing landscape of the workplace.

It was in those moments of compromise, when they acknowledged their own limitations and embraced the strengths of their colleagues, that they truly began to understand the power of a team. It wasn't about surrendering to the demands of others; it was about finding a common ground, a shared path that led to a better outcome for everyone.

The office had become a microcosm of society, a reflection of the challenges and opportunities that we all face in our daily lives. It was a reminder that cooperation, understanding, and a sense of humor could go a long way in overcoming obstacles and achieving common goals.

And as they continued to navigate the complexities of their shared work environment, they realized that the art of compromise was not just a tool for managing chaos; it was the foundation for building a truly harmonious and productive workplace.

Looking to the Future

The air in the office buzzed with a newfound energy. The lingering scent of coffee and the faint echoes of laughter filled the space, a testament to the transformation that had taken place. Gone were the days of frantic emails, overflowing inboxes, and endless rounds of unproductive meetings. In their place stood a sense of camaraderie, a shared understanding of the importance of collaboration, and a genuine appreciation for each other's unique quirks. It was a far cry from the tumultuous journey they had endured, but it was a journey that had ultimately brought them closer together.

The procrastinator, once notorious for his eleventh-hour sprints and last-minute apologies, now embraced a sense of responsibility, his deadlines met with a newfound efficiency. The office drama queen, whose penchant for gossip had threatened to consume the very fabric of their workplace, had found a new outlet for her theatrical flair – organizing team-building activities that fostered genuine connection rather than manufactured drama.

The team celebrated their successes, recognizing that even the smallest victories were hard-won, a testament to their newfound ability to work together. They remembered the days of frantic deadlines and unfulfilled promises, the times when they had felt overwhelmed and frustrated. They had faced those challenges head-on, not with a sense of dread but with a shared determination to overcome them.

They were no longer just colleagues; they were a team, united by a shared goal of creating a positive and productive work environment. They had learned that humor, empathy, and a willingness to compromise were not just niceties, but essential ingredients in building a strong and cohesive team. They had discovered that a little bit of laughter could go a long way in diffusing tension, fostering collaboration, and reminding them that even in the most stressful of situations, there was always room for a bit of lightheartedness.

The office had become a place where creativity blossomed, where ideas were exchanged freely, and where everyone felt valued and respected. They had learned to appreciate the strengths of their colleagues, understanding that each individual brought something unique to the table. They celebrated their differences, recognizing that diversity was a source of strength and innovation.

As they looked toward the future, they did so with a sense of hope and determination. The challenges they had faced had been formidable, but they had overcome them. They had learned valuable lessons about teamwork, communication, and the importance of finding common ground. They knew that there would be new challenges ahead, but they were confident that they could face them together. They had built a foundation of trust, respect, and camaraderie that would serve them well in the years to come.

They had wrangle the wreckage of their once chaotic office, and in the process, they had discovered something even more valuable: a sense of belonging, a feeling of unity, and a shared purpose.

The once-dreaded office had become a place where they thrived, where they learned, and where they grew together. It was a testament to the power of teamwork, the resilience of the human spirit, and the undeniable truth that even in the most chaotic of environments, a little bit of humor, a lot of empathy, and a whole lot of collaboration could make all the difference.

Embracing Change

The air in the office hummed with an almost tangible energy. It wasn't the usual, pre-deadline buzz, the kind that made everyone's coffee mugs rattle and their fingers fly across keyboards. No, this was something different, a spark of genuine excitement and optimism that had been dormant for far too long. It was like the sun finally breaking through after weeks of relentless rain, casting a warm glow on everyone's faces.

The recent chaos had been a catalyst, a crucible of sorts. The team, once a collection of individual cogs in the corporate machine, had been forged together by the shared experience of near-meltdown. They had faced down the abyss of office pandemonium and emerged, not unscathed, but with a newfound appreciation for the simple pleasures of a functional office environment.

This newfound appreciation was evident in the way they approached their work, a subtle shift in their collective mindset. The procrastinator, once known for his last-minute bursts of frantic energy, found himself taking on tasks with newfound enthusiasm, a proactive approach that surprised even himself. The gossip queen, once a purveyor of office drama, had discovered the power of constructive feedback, channeling her energy into positive conversations that fostered collaboration.

This wasn't just a temporary change, a fleeting sense of unity in the face of adversity. It was a genuine evolution, a transformation that had roots in the shared struggles they had overcome. They had learned to see the value in each other, the unique strengths and perspectives that made them a team, not just a collection of individuals.

Change, they had discovered, could be a powerful force, a catalyst for growth and self-discovery. It wasn't always easy, but it was always worth it. The office, once a hotbed of frustration and tension, now buzzed with a different kind of energy, a contagious energy that spread like wildfire.

As they navigated the new landscape of their transformed workspace, they found themselves embracing challenges with a renewed sense of purpose. They had learned that even the most seemingly insurmountable obstacles could be overcome with teamwork, humor, and a healthy dose of optimism.

One afternoon, a new challenge arose, a project that required innovative solutions and a collaborative approach. It was a complex undertaking, one that would test their newfound unity and require them to draw on all their combined strengths.

At first, there were whispers of apprehension, a hint of doubt that lingered in the air. But quickly, a collective spirit of determination emerged. They had faced down the office apocalypse, survived the chaos, and learned from their mistakes. They knew that, together, they could overcome anything.

"This is our chance to prove that we're not just a bunch of misfits, but a team of innovators," declared the procrastinator, his newfound enthusiasm surprisingly genuine.

"And we're going to do it with style, of course," added the gossip queen, her voice laced with a hint of mischief.

The team huddled, their heads buzzing with ideas. They brainstormed, debated, and challenged each other in a way that was both constructive and humorous. The energy in the room was electric, fueled by a shared passion for success and a desire to prove that their transformation was genuine.

As they worked, they discovered that their individual quirks, once seen as liabilities, were actually valuable assets. The procrastinator's ability to think outside the box brought fresh perspectives to the table. The gossip queen's knack for connecting with people helped to build consensus and foster a sense of shared purpose.

They embraced the challenges, not with fear, but with excitement. They learned to appreciate the unique strengths of each team member, recognizing that their individual differences were what made them a powerful force.

The project, once a looming threat, became an opportunity, a chance to demonstrate their newfound unity and showcase their combined talents. It was a chance to prove that they weren't just surviving, but thriving in the face of change.

And as they worked, they realized that the greatest reward wasn't just the successful completion of the project, but the journey they shared, the bond that had been forged in the crucible of chaos. They had discovered that change, when embraced with optimism and enthusiasm, could lead to unexpected opportunities for growth, collaboration, and personal fulfillment.

The Innovation Challenge

The office, once a haven of predictable monotony, had morphed into a breeding ground for unexpected chaos. The "Innovation Challenge" – a company-wide competition urging employees to devise groundbreaking ideas – was the latest catalyst for this seismic shift. The initial announcement, brimming with promises of hefty rewards and glowing recognition, had stirred excitement within the ranks. But as the deadline loomed, so did the reality of the challenge.

The task itself wasn't inherently daunting. The problem, however, lay in the very people tasked with solving it. Our office wasn't exactly a hub of brilliant innovators. It was a collective of endearingly flawed individuals, each with their own peculiar brand of dysfunctionality.

Take Harold, the self-proclaimed "idea machine." Harold was a master of generating concepts, but his execution was a disaster waiting to happen. His ideas, while audacious, were often impractical, like suggesting we replace the office coffee machine with a self-replicating bean-producing device.

Then there was Penelope, the resident cynic. Penelope, with her perpetually skeptical demeanor, viewed the challenge as a pointless exercise in corporate manipulation. She scoffed at the notion of innovation, muttering under her breath about "smoke and mirrors" and "hollow promises."

And let's not forget the office manager, Mrs. Henderson, a woman whose love for routine rivaled her obsession with staplers. Any deviation from the established office protocol was anathema to her, and the Innovation Challenge felt like a direct assault on her meticulously crafted system.

The initial stages of the challenge were marked by a flurry of ill-conceived brainstorming sessions. Harold's ideas were met with blank stares, Penelope's cynicism poisoned the air, and Mrs. Henderson's stern glares kept everyone from venturing beyond the confines of the office handbook. It was a recipe for disaster, and disaster, it seemed, was always the main course at our office.

But amidst the chaos, a glimmer of hope emerged. The office's resident procrastinator, the perpetually late and perpetually unorganized Emily, had a peculiar talent. Emily thrived in chaos. She saw opportunities where others saw roadblocks. And while she might not have been the most organized person, she possessed a remarkable ability to connect disparate ideas, weaving together the most improbable solutions.

Emily's approach was unorthodox. Instead of meticulously planning and organizing, she embraced the spontaneous and the messy. She threw herself into the heart of the chaos, embracing its unpredictable energy, and somehow, miraculously, she started to see the challenge through a different lens.

As Emily delved deeper into the Innovation Challenge, she stumbled upon an overlooked opportunity. The company, in its zeal to promote the competition, had neglected to provide employees with adequate resources. There was a lack of access to research materials, funding for prototypes, and even basic equipment. Emily saw this as a chance to create something truly innovative – not a groundbreaking product, but a system that would empower employees to innovate, a system that would dismantle the barriers to creativity.

Emily's idea was bold and daring. She proposed building an internal innovation hub, a space where employees could collaborate, share ideas, and access resources. It would be a space where the "creative misfits" of the office, like Harold and Penelope, could channel their energy into something productive.

At first, the idea was met with skepticism. Mrs. Henderson raised concerns about the budgetary implications and the potential for disruptions to the established office flow. Harold, in his usual fashion, proposed an even more elaborate plan, involving a futuristic holographic projection room. Penelope, as always, was quick to point out the flaws in Emily's concept.

But Emily, with her uncanny ability to navigate chaos, persisted. She presented her plan with infectious enthusiasm, showcasing the potential of her idea to empower employees and foster a culture of innovation. She even managed to win over Penelope, who grudgingly admitted that the concept had merit.

The office was abuzz with activity as they gathered to brainstorm the design of the innovation hub. Harold, surprisingly, contributed some practical ideas, though he couldn't resist adding a few "futuristic" embellishments. Penelope, despite her initial reluctance, offered valuable insights, identifying potential roadblocks and suggesting solutions. Even Mrs. Henderson, who had initially opposed the idea, found herself drawn into the creative process, her meticulous planning and organizational skills proving invaluable to the endeavor.

The creation of the innovation hub marked a turning point for the office. It wasn't a perfect system, there were still hiccups and mishaps, but it had breathed new life into the workplace. Employees, once stuck in their routines, were now energized by the opportunity to create and collaborate. The office had found a new rhythm, a more dynamic and creative one.

The Innovation Challenge had tested the office, exposing its flaws and pushing its limits. But it had also unearthed a hidden potential, a collective spirit of ingenuity that had been waiting to be unleashed. The challenge had transformed the office from a stagnant pool of mediocrity to a dynamic ecosystem of innovation, all thanks to the unconventional and unorthodox approach of Emily, the office's most unexpected hero.

Unlikely Leaders

The innovation challenge was unlike anything they had encountered before. It wasn't a matter of cleaning up messes or navigating office politics, but a real test of their collective ingenuity. The project was a game-changer, a chance to rewrite the company's future, but it was also a daunting task that required a level of collaboration they had only glimpsed in the aftermath of their office-wide chaos.

The initial meetings were a flurry of ideas, some brilliant, others bordering on absurd. It was as if the office had become a brainstorming factory, churning out concepts at a dizzying pace. But as the days turned into weeks, a sense of frustration began to creep in. They were all pulling in different directions, their energy scattering like a pack of startled pigeons.

Then, something unexpected happened. It wasn't a grand epiphany or a sudden burst of inspiration; it was a simple act of empathy. Emily, the perpetual procrastinator who had once thrived on the last-minute chaos, noticed the growing tension in the team. She saw the furrowed brows, the tense shoulders, and the way everyone seemed to be holding their breath.

She decided to do something about it. She started by bringing in a giant, inflatable rubber chicken. It wasn't exactly a conventional team-building exercise, but it did the trick. Laughter filled the room, easing the tension and reminding everyone that they were in this together.

It was the catalyst they needed. Emily, who had once been the epitome of disorganization, became the unexpected leader, her humor and empathy bridging the gaps that had formed between her colleagues. Her unconventional methods, fueled by her innate understanding of their shared struggles, brought them together in a way no formal meeting or brainstorming session ever could.

Even Michael, the office drama queen who had previously thrived on gossip and conflict, found himself drawn to Emily's leadership. He realized that his own brand of drama was no longer serving him. He was tired of being the center of attention, tired of stirring the pot. He wanted to be a part of something bigger, something positive.

Together, Emily and Michael formed an unlikely partnership. Emily, the champion of chaos, brought the humor and the empathy, while Michael, the master of manipulation, brought his keen understanding of human psychology. They worked together, navigating the minefield of office dynamics, encouraging collaboration and defusing potential conflict with a mix of laughter and shrewd observation.

The rest of the team, seeing the transformation in their two most chaotic colleagues, started to follow suit. They realized that the innovation challenge was not just about coming up with a brilliant idea, but about working together, supporting each other, and finding common ground.

As they delved deeper into the project, they discovered that their differences were not weaknesses but strengths. The procrastinator's ability to think outside the box, the drama queen's knack for reading people, and the meticulous planner's attention to detail all came together to create a unique and powerful force.

The project, initially a source of stress and anxiety, became a source of pride and accomplishment. The team was working better than ever before, their laughter echoing through the hallways, their energy focused and productive. They were no longer just colleagues; they were a team, united by their shared experience and their newfound appreciation for the power of empathy and humor.

As they presented their final proposal, they could see the surprise and admiration in the eyes of their superiors. They had not only met the challenge; they had exceeded it, proving that even the most chaotic team could achieve greatness when they learned to embrace their differences and work together with a shared purpose.

The innovation challenge was a turning point for the entire office. It marked a shift from a culture of chaos and conflict to a culture of collaboration and creativity. The team, once defined by its messy habits and petty rivalries, had become a beacon of positive change. And at the heart of it all, the unlikely leaders, Emily and Michael, stood as testaments to the power of humor, empathy, and the unexpected ways in which people can come together to achieve extraordinary things.

The Role of Humor

The office had undergone a remarkable transformation. Gone were the days of overflowing inboxes, misplaced files, and endless gossip sessions. In their place stood a team united by a shared sense of purpose, a newfound appreciation for collaboration, and, of course, a healthy dose of humor.

Humor had always been a crucial part of the office dynamics, serving as a coping mechanism for the relentless chaos that had once reigned. It was the invisible thread that connected the team, allowing them to laugh in the face of adversity and find solace in shared experiences. It acted like a safety valve, releasing pressure and preventing tension from building up to explosive levels.

The power of laughter was evident in the way they navigated even the most mundane tasks. Meetings that once felt like interminable trials now unfolded with unexpected bursts of humor. A misplaced document, a forgotten deadline, or an awkward email exchange – all became fodder for lighthearted banter, defusing potential conflict and creating a sense of shared amusement.

One particularly memorable moment occurred during a company-wide presentation. As the presenter, a seasoned professional known for his dry wit, stumbled over his words and fumbled with his slides, the audience, instead of cringing with embarrassment, erupted in laughter. The presenter, caught off guard, joined in the mirth, breaking the tension and transforming the situation into a light-hearted moment.

It was through these shared laughs that the team forged a deeper understanding of one another. Humor became a bridge, connecting colleagues who had once been distant or even hostile. It created a sense of camaraderie, allowing them to relate to each other on a personal level and appreciate their individual quirks.

But humor was not just about laughter. It was also a powerful tool for fostering creativity and innovation. When faced with a challenge, the team would often turn to their sense of humor to find creative solutions. It was a way to step back from the problem, see it from a different perspective, and generate fresh ideas.

One particularly challenging project required the team to develop a new marketing campaign for a niche product. As they brainstormed ideas, frustration mounted, and the team seemed to be hitting a wall. But then, someone cracked a joke about the product's unique features, and suddenly the mood shifted. The laughter sparked a chain reaction of creative ideas, leading to a campaign that was both innovative and successful.

Humor had become an integral part of the office's DNA, a shared language that helped them navigate the ups and downs of work life. It was a testament to the power of laughter to bring people together, build trust, and unlock creative potential.

In a world where work could often feel like an uphill battle, humor became a beacon of hope, reminding the team that even amidst the chaos, they could find moments of joy, connection, and inspiration. It was a reminder that even in the most stressful situations, a shared laugh could go a long way.

New Beginnings

The air in the office felt different. Lighter. Less thick with the scent of anxiety and dread that had permeated the cubicles for months. Instead, a fresh, almost optimistic energy buzzed in the air, propelled by the shared sense of accomplishment that had settled over the team. The disastrous clean-up operation, the constant stream of office drama, the frantic attempts to wrangle the wreckage – all those chaotic episodes seemed to have finally faded into a hazy, humorous memory.

The office, once a battleground of clashing personalities and conflicting workstyles, now held a sense of camaraderie. The team had learned a valuable lesson: even the most disorganized, chaotic group could find a semblance of order and harmony, provided they were willing to work together, laugh at their mistakes, and recognize their strengths.

"This is actually… bearable," whispered Emily, the office manager, to Sarah, the resident bookworm, as they passed each other in the hallway, a faint smile playing on Emily's lips.

"It's a miracle, isn't it?" Sarah replied, shaking her head in disbelief. "Who knew we could function without a daily dose of office chaos?"

Even the office's resident procrastinator, Mark, seemed to have undergone a metamorphosis. Gone were the last-minute frantic rushes, the caffeine-fueled all-nighters, and the panicked apologies. In his place was a slightly more organized, slightly more composed version of himself, a phenomenon that left his colleagues bewildered and, strangely enough, relieved.

"I think I finally figured out the secret to getting things done," Mark declared to his colleagues, his voice laced with a hint of self-satisfaction. "It's all about working on things… ahead of time."

The team erupted in laughter, a sound that resonated through the office with a sense of genuine joy.

The transformation wasn't just about the work. The office's social scene had also undergone a notable shift. The lunchtime gatherings, once characterized by tense silences and awkward exchanges, were now filled with lively conversation, shared jokes, and the occasional impromptu dance-off.

One afternoon, the office's resident drama queen, Melissa, even initiated a team-building exercise, surprising everyone with a series of hilarious and surprisingly insightful icebreakers.

"I think I've learned that office gossip is a double-edged sword," Melissa declared to the group, a hint of self-awareness in her voice. "It can bring you down, or it can… make you laugh. I think I prefer the latter."

Her colleagues, who had long since grown weary of her gossiping, erupted in applause.

The change in the office had not gone unnoticed by their boss, Mr. Thompson, a stern and demanding man who had long since grown accustomed to the office's chaotic rhythm. He couldn't quite pinpoint the exact shift, but he knew something was different.

"The office feels… lighter," he mused to his assistant, a thoughtful frown etched on his face.

"It's like a weight has been lifted," she agreed, a smile brightening her face.

One Tuesday morning, Mr. Thompson announced a new challenge: the company was launching a new product line and needed the team to come up with a fresh marketing campaign. The announcement sent a ripple of nervous excitement through the office. While the team had successfully weathered past storms, this new challenge felt different.

"This is our chance to prove that we're not just a group of misfits," said Sarah, her voice filled with determination. "We're a team, and we can do this!"

And with that, the team plunged into the marketing campaign with renewed vigor. They brainstormed, debated, argued, and laughed their way through endless hours of meetings, their collective energy fuelled by a newfound sense of purpose and a shared desire to succeed.

But the journey wouldn't be without its bumps. The marketing campaign was complex, and the team faced its share of setbacks. There were disagreements, unexpected delays, and the occasional outburst of frustration.

"This is just like the old days," muttered Mark, his voice filled with a hint of nostalgia. "Except now, we actually have a plan."

The team's laughter echoed through the office.

"We've learned to embrace the chaos," said Emily, a twinkle in her eye. "But we've also learned how to work together, and that's what really matters."

The team was determined to succeed, and they were prepared to face any challenge that came their way, armed with their newfound skills and the shared humor that had become their secret weapon.

Recognizing Contributions

The office was abuzz with a newfound energy, a collective sense of accomplishment that permeated the air like a fragrant, freshly brewed pot of coffee. It wasn't just the lingering scent of freshly polished desks and sanitized keyboards; it was the palpable feeling that they, the once chaotic band of office misfits, had somehow wrung a semblance of order from their previously tumultuous environment.

The transformation wasn't a sudden, magical metamorphosis. It had been a long, arduous journey, marked by a series of mishaps, near-meltdowns, and a few too many coffee-stained reports. But through it all, they had learned, grown, and ultimately, discovered the unexpected power of teamwork.

It was a far cry from the days when the office was ruled by the whims of the procrastinator, whose desk looked like a bomb had exploded in a library, and the office gossip queen, whose endless whispering had the power to incite a full-blown office war.

Now, the procrastinator, who used to thrive on the adrenaline rush of last-minute deadlines, had become a surprisingly efficient contributor, his newfound sense of urgency fueled by the collective energy of his colleagues. The gossip queen, her voice no longer a weapon of mass distraction, was now a source of unexpected insights, her sharp wit employed to defuse tension and bring a touch of humor to even the most mundane tasks.

The team had found its rhythm. They had learned the importance of clear communication, the value of sharing the workload, and the unexpected power of laughter to melt away even the most persistent office anxieties. They had discovered that even the most chaotic situations could be navigated, if not mastered, with a healthy dose of empathy and a shared commitment to achieving a common goal.

There were still moments, of course, when the old chaos threatened to resurface. A misplaced memo, a forgotten meeting, or a misplaced stapler could throw the best-laid plans into disarray. But now, instead of succumbing to panic, they met these challenges with a shared sense of humor, knowing that they had the strength and the resilience to overcome even the most unexpected obstacles.

This wasn't simply about the office, it was about them, the individuals who had found themselves united in the face of chaos. They had grown closer, discovering hidden talents, unexpected strengths, and a shared passion for making their little corner of the world, their office, a place where they could not only survive, but thrive.

Each member of the team had made their own unique contribution to this transformation. The office manager, once a prisoner of her own meticulousness, had learned to let go, embrace the imperfection, and trust her colleagues to do their best. The creative director, once a lone wolf, had discovered the joy of collaboration, realizing that a team effort could produce something even more powerful than individual genius.

They had become a team, not simply because they shared a common workplace, but because they had learned to appreciate each other's strengths, embrace each other's weaknesses, and celebrate the collective power of their individual contributions.

And so, the office that was once a breeding ground for chaos
and dysfunction had become a haven of collaboration and
camaraderie. It was a testament to the power of teamwork,
the transformative magic of empathy, and the enduring
strength of the human spirit, even in the most chaotic of
office environments.

This new era wasn't about perfect harmony or a utopian
office utopia. It was about acknowledging that imperfections
were inevitable, that chaos was a natural part of life, and that
even in the most challenging of situations, there was always
room for laughter, learning, and a shared commitment to
making the workplace a place where everyone could feel
valued, appreciated, and empowered.

The office was still a place of deadlines, meetings, and
occasional office dramas, but it was also a place where they
had learned to embrace the messy reality of work life,
knowing that even in the midst of chaos, there was always
the potential for growth, connection, and even a little bit of
fun.

The journey from chaos to collaboration had been an
unexpected adventure. They had discovered the true
meaning of teamwork, not just as a concept, but as a living,
breathing entity that had the power to transform their lives,
their work, and their perspectives.

As they navigated the ever-changing landscape of the office,
they did so with a newfound confidence, knowing that
whatever challenges lay ahead, they were ready to face them
together, with a collective spirit that had been forged in the
fires of chaos and emerged, stronger and more resilient than
ever before.

Forging Stronger Bonds

The shared journey of wrangling the wreckage had forged an unexpected bond among the colleagues. What had started as a series of haphazard attempts to restore order had morphed into a testament to the power of shared experiences, laughter, and the realization that even the most chaotic work environment could benefit from a touch of human connection.

The office potluck, once a source of stress and food-related disasters, now seemed like a distant memory. They had navigated the treacherous waters of the annual performance review cycle, emerging with a newfound understanding of each other's strengths and weaknesses. The procrastinator, once a symbol of chaos, had surprised everyone with his unexpected bursts of efficiency. The drama queen, who had thrived on gossip and office intrigue, had discovered a surprising sense of empathy.

There were moments of frustration, of course, where the old habits threatened to resurface. There were times when the pressure of deadlines and the endless stream of emails threatened to drown them in a sea of disarray. But through it all, they had learned to rely on each other. They had learned to communicate, to compromise, and to laugh in the face of adversity.

The office, once a battleground of egos and miscommunication, had transformed into a place of shared purpose and mutual respect. The walls that had once seemed to divide them had crumbled, replaced by a sense of camaraderie that extended beyond the confines of the cubicle walls.

One particularly challenging project, a cross-departmental collaboration that threatened to implode under the weight of conflicting deadlines and personalities, became a pivotal turning point. They faced insurmountable obstacles, a seemingly endless stream of unexpected challenges, and a mountain of work that seemed impossible to conquer. Yet, fueled by a shared sense of purpose and a growing trust in one another, they persevered. They rallied around each other, offered support, and celebrated even the smallest victories.

In the midst of the chaos, laughter became a lifeline. They found humor in the absurdity of their situation, turning their frustrations into inside jokes that only they could understand. The procrastinator, now a reformed character, found himself the unlikely source of comic relief, his witty observations and dry humor easing the tension. The drama queen, with her newfound empathy, became a master of reading the room, sensing when a lighthearted quip was needed to lighten the mood.

The office, once a place where they dreaded coming to work, now felt like a sanctuary. They were a team, united not by a shared love for spreadsheets or a thirst for corporate success, but by their shared experiences, their vulnerabilities, and their ability to find humor in the face of adversity.

The shared journey had forged a bond that extended beyond the office walls. They had become friends, a group of individuals who had discovered the power of empathy, the strength of collaboration, and the importance of laughter in a world where chaos often threatened to prevail. They had learned that even in the most disorganized workplace, a sense of community and a shared understanding could transform the seemingly insurmountable into a source of strength, unity, and laughter.

As they celebrated the completion of their latest project, a monumental achievement that had once seemed impossible, they raised their glasses, not to success, but to the unlikely bonds they had forged in the face of chaos. They had learned that the most valuable asset in any workplace, even one as chaotic as theirs, was not productivity or efficiency, but the human connection that allowed them to navigate the most difficult challenges and emerge stronger, together.

This realization, born from their shared journey of wrangling the wreckage, was a testament to the power of shared experiences, the transformative power of laughter, and the unexpected bonds that could emerge from the most unlikely of places. They had learned that even in the face of chaos, humor and human connection could pave the way for a more harmonious, productive, and fulfilling workplace.

Overcoming Setbacks

The office had settled into a rhythm, a new kind of harmony that felt almost surreal after the chaotic months that had passed. The team, once a collection of mismatched personalities, had learned to navigate each other's quirks, to anticipate the inevitable office snafus, and to work together to overcome the unexpected. But even in the midst of this newfound harmony, there were whispers of a looming challenge, a new obstacle on the horizon that threatened to disrupt their carefully cultivated peace.

It started with a series of mishaps, each seemingly insignificant on its own, but cumulatively suggesting that something was amiss. The coffee machine, which had been a source of constant consternation throughout the previous months, inexplicably started spewing out lukewarm, bitter concoctions. The company-wide email system, which had recently been upgraded to a state-of-the-art platform, began sending out nonsensical spam, prompting bewildered recipients to question their sanity. And then there was the office plant, a large, leafy fern that had somehow managed to survive even the most neglectful of caretakers, which inexplicably started wilting.

These were mere annoyances, nothing compared to the trials they'd faced before. But there was something about the air, a subtle shift in the atmosphere, that made the team uneasy. They exchanged anxious glances, wondering if this was the prelude to another chaotic chapter, another tumultuous journey through the unpredictable waters of office life.

It was Sarah, the resident worrier, who finally voiced the unspoken fear. "Do you think this is the start of something big?" she asked, her voice laced with a mix of apprehension and morbid curiosity.

"Oh, Sarah, always the drama queen," chuckled Mark, the office jokester, who seemed to thrive on the unpredictable. "It's just a few minor setbacks, nothing a little teamwork and a whole lot of coffee can't fix."

But beneath his lighthearted facade, even Mark couldn't shake the feeling that something was brewing, something bigger than a few malfunctioning machines and a dying fern. And as the days unfolded, his intuition was confirmed.

The office, once a bastion of relative peace, began to teeter on the brink of chaos once again. The printer, a notorious troublemaker in its own right, decided to completely shut down, refusing to spit out even a single page. The internet connection, a vital lifeline in the digital age, became so unreliable that it felt like the office was on the verge of being plunged back into the dark ages. And as if these weren't enough, the company's annual performance review cycle was rapidly approaching, a dreaded event that always seemed to amplify the office's anxieties.

The atmosphere grew thick with tension. The usual banter and lighthearted exchanges were replaced by hushed whispers and anxious glances. The once vibrant, chaotic energy of the office had been replaced by a pervasive sense of dread. It felt as if they were back in the early days of their shared ordeal, on the precipice of another chaotic freefall.

"This is insane," groaned Michael, the office manager, whose perpetually calm demeanor had started to fray under the strain of the escalating chaos. "Just when I thought we were finally on the right track, things go haywire again."

But the team, seasoned by their shared experiences, knew better than to succumb to despair. They had already weathered the storms of office anarchy, and they weren't about to crumble now.

"Remember, it's not the problems themselves that define us, it's how we respond to them," said Lisa, the team's resident optimist, her voice a beacon of calm in the storm. "We've faced bigger challenges before, and we've always come out stronger on the other side. This too shall pass."

Her words were a reminder of the lessons they'd learned: that teamwork could overcome almost any obstacle, that humor could diffuse even the most tense situations, and that the power of resilience resided within each of them.

And so, they gathered in a huddle, their faces a mix of determination and nervous anticipation. They shared a collective sigh, acknowledging the gravity of their situation, but also recognizing the strength they found in each other. This wasn't just another office challenge; it was an opportunity to prove to themselves, and to the world, that they could overcome any hurdle thrown their way, that their bond, forged in the fires of chaos, was stronger than ever before.

As they launched into their usual game plan – a mix of problem-solving, witty observations, and an abundance of dark humor – they knew they would face their challenges head-on, with a collective spirit that had grown stronger through the trials they'd shared. The chaos was inevitable, but they were ready to wrangle it, together.

Their journey wasn't a linear progression, a smooth sail towards a utopia of organized desks and perfectly timed deadlines. It was a messy, chaotic dance, a constant battle between the desire for order and the inevitable onslaught of disruptions.

But as they navigated this unpredictable landscape, they discovered something deeper than just an office. They found a shared purpose, a sense of belonging, and a resilience that went beyond the walls of their workplace.

Each setback was a learning experience, each hurdle a chance to strengthen their bonds. They learned to embrace the chaos, to find humor in the midst of frustration, and to rely on each other for support. They were a team, not just by circumstance, but by choice, a band of misfits united by a shared experience and a desire to create something better, something more.

The setbacks, even as they threatened to unravel their carefully constructed progress, were ultimately what made them stronger. They were the fuel that powered their resilience, the trials that tested their limits and revealed their true strengths.

And as they faced each new challenge, the laughter echoed through the office, a testament to their unwavering spirit, a reminder that even in the midst of chaos, they would find a way to wrangle the wreckage, together.

The Importance of Empathy

The office had become a symphony of camaraderie, a testament to the power of shared struggles and the healing touch of laughter. The once-fractured team, each member a unique instrument playing their own discordant tune, had found a rhythm together. But even in this newfound harmony, a subtle dissonance remained. It was the quiet whispers of frustration, the unspoken anxieties, the moments when someone felt unseen or unheard. This was the challenge that lay before them, the final note to be played in their evolving symphony: empathy.

Empathy, in its simplest form, is the ability to understand and share the feelings of another. In the workplace, it's the unspoken language of respect, the bridge that connects colleagues across the chasm of individual anxieties and frustrations. It's the willingness to step outside of your own immediate concerns and see the world from another's perspective. In a world where every employee is a cog in a machine, empathy is the oil that keeps the gears turning smoothly.

Imagine a team where everyone is so focused on their own goals that they lose sight of the bigger picture. Imagine the constant pressure to perform, the endless stream of deadlines, the fear of falling behind. It's easy to get caught in a cycle of self-preservation, where empathy is a luxury you simply can't afford. But this myopic view, this tunnel vision of self-interest, is precisely what can lead to a breakdown in communication, a breakdown in teamwork, and ultimately, a breakdown in productivity.

Empathy is not a weakness; it's a strength. It's the ability to acknowledge the human side of work, to recognize that each colleague is an individual with their own unique set of challenges, goals, and aspirations. It's about creating a work environment where vulnerability is not a sign of weakness but a sign of strength, where everyone feels safe enough to be their authentic selves.

But empathy is not simply about feeling sorry for someone; it's about understanding their situation, their perspective, their needs. It's about listening without judgment, offering support without condescension. It's about acknowledging their efforts, celebrating their achievements, and providing encouragement when they face setbacks.

Think about the most supportive colleagues you've ever worked with. What made them stand out? Was it their ability to make you feel heard? Was it their willingness to offer a helping hand when you were struggling? Was it their genuine interest in your well-being? These are the qualities of empathetic individuals, those who create a positive and supportive work environment.

Let's take a look at how empathy can be implemented in a real-world office setting:

The Procrastinator's Perspective:

Remember our beloved procrastinator? He's the king of last-minute rushes, the champion of eleventh-hour heroics. He thrives on chaos, his adrenaline pumping with every ticking clock. But what if we viewed his procrastination not as a character flaw but as a symptom of something deeper? Perhaps he's struggling with anxiety, overwhelmed by the sheer volume of tasks, or battling a fear of failure.

Empathy towards the procrastinator might involve understanding his underlying fears and anxieties. It might involve offering him a gentle nudge toward organization, a helping hand to break down large tasks into manageable steps, or simply a patient ear when he's feeling overwhelmed. It's about building trust and creating an environment where he feels comfortable seeking help without fear of judgment.

The Gossip Queen's Redemption:

The office drama queen, fueled by gossip and fueled by a need to feel important. Her actions might seem like a distraction, a threat to workplace harmony. But empathy requires looking beyond the surface. Perhaps she's feeling insecure, seeking validation, or simply longing for connection. She might be using gossip as a way to cope with her own anxieties or to feel part of something bigger than herself.

Empathy towards the gossip queen might involve addressing her underlying needs for validation and belonging. It might involve redirecting her energy towards positive interactions, offering her opportunities to contribute in meaningful ways, or simply reminding her of the power of kindness and respect. It's about helping her find a more constructive way to express her need for connection and validation.

Building a Culture of Empathy:

Empathy is not a one-time act; it's an ongoing process. It's about creating a culture where everyone feels valued, respected, and supported. Here are a few tips for fostering a more empathetic workplace:

Active Listening: Make an effort to truly listen to your colleagues when they speak. Pay attention to their body language, their tone, and their words. Try to understand their perspective, even if you don't agree with it.

Open Communication: Encourage open and honest communication. Create a safe space for colleagues to share their concerns, their challenges, and their ideas without fear of judgment.

Empathy in Action: Look for opportunities to help your colleagues, even in small ways. Offer to help them with a project, share your expertise, or simply lend an ear.

Celebrate Successes: Recognize and celebrate the achievements of your colleagues. Let them know that you appreciate their contributions and their efforts.

Seek Feedback: Ask for feedback from your colleagues on how you can improve your communication and your approach. Be open to constructive criticism and be willing to learn and grow.

Empathy is not just about being nice; it's about building a more productive, positive, and fulfilling work environment for everyone. It's about creating a team where everyone feels valued, respected, and empowered to do their best work.

In the grand symphony of the office, empathy is the conductor, the one who brings all the instruments together in perfect harmony. It's the key to creating a workplace where everyone can truly thrive.

The Teams Legacy

As the office settled into a new rhythm, a sense of accomplishment hung in the air, like the lingering scent of freshly brewed coffee after a particularly productive meeting. The transformation was palpable. The once-cluttered breakroom now gleamed with order, the overflowing filing cabinets stood at attention, and even the office plants seemed to have perked up, their leaves reaching for the sun with newfound enthusiasm. It was as if the collective effort to wrangle the wreckage had infused the very walls with a spirit of optimism.

The team, once a collection of mismatched personalities prone to chaos, had become a force to be reckoned with, a band of unlikely heroes who had stared into the abyss of disorganization and emerged victorious. The procrastinator, once the embodiment of last-minute panic, had found a newfound sense of purpose, his deadlines no longer looming over him like a thundercloud. The drama queen, her gossip-fueled flames extinguished, had discovered the power of positive communication, replacing her penchant for spreading rumors with genuine interest in her colleagues' well-being.

Their journey had been a roller coaster ride of mishaps, frustrations, and moments of utter despair. Yet, through it all, humor had remained their steadfast companion. It was the laughter that had kept them going, the shared chuckles that had defused tension and brought them together. Each disastrous scheme, each unforeseen obstacle, each moment of utter chaos, had become a shared experience, a bonding ritual that forged an unbreakable connection between them.

They had learned the value of communication, the power of collaboration, and the importance of empathy. They had discovered that even the most dysfunctional of teams could find a path to harmony, and that the journey itself, with all its twists and turns, was a testament to their resilience and their shared spirit.

But the legacy they had created extended beyond the walls of their office. They had proven that change was possible, that even the most entrenched habits could be broken, and that a little bit of humor could go a long way in navigating the complexities of workplace dynamics. Their story was a reminder that every team, regardless of its quirks and flaws, had the potential to achieve greatness, one laugh, one shared triumph, one act of kindness at a time.

The transformation wasn't just about tidying up desks and organizing paperwork. It was about redefining what it meant to be a team. It was about recognizing the individual strengths that each member brought to the table, and celebrating those differences, rather than allowing them to create division.

They had learned the importance of acknowledging each other's contributions, big or small. The procrastinator, for instance, had a knack for finding creative solutions in the face of impending deadlines. The drama queen, with her unparalleled social skills, became the office's unofficial morale booster, her gossiping tendencies now channeled into building genuine connections with her colleagues.

Their journey had taught them that even in the face of adversity, there was always room for laughter. Laughter, they had realized, was not just a way to alleviate stress, but a powerful tool for building relationships, fostering empathy, and creating a sense of shared purpose.

The legacy they left behind was not just a clean office and a smoothly functioning team. It was a testament to the power of human connection, the ability to learn from mistakes, and the transformative potential of shared laughter.

As they looked ahead, they did so with a newfound sense of confidence and optimism. They had faced their demons, embraced their quirks, and emerged as a stronger, more cohesive unit. They had learned to navigate the complexities of human relationships, to appreciate the value of diverse perspectives, and to find humor even in the most chaotic of situations.

The office they had transformed was no longer just a workplace. It was a haven, a sanctuary where they could be themselves, where their individual talents were celebrated, and where their shared journey had forged an unbreakable bond.

Their story served as an inspiration to other teams, a reminder that even the most chaotic of workplaces could be transformed, one laughter, one shared triumph, one act of kindness at a time. They had proven that even in the most dysfunctional of environments, a spirit of collaboration, a sense of humor, and a willingness to embrace each other's quirks could lead to a truly remarkable transformation.

A New Vision

The office, once a breeding ground for chaos, had begun to resemble a well-oiled machine. The air hung heavy with a newfound sense of accomplishment, a testament to the team's shared journey through the wreckage. The constant barrage of procrastination, gossip, and general disarray had been wrestled into submission, replaced by a collaborative spirit that hummed with a quiet confidence.

The transformation had been gradual, a slow burn of self-discovery and shared purpose. They had learned to navigate the treacherous waters of office dynamics, using humor as their compass and teamwork as their anchor. Their laughter, once born from frustration, now echoed with camaraderie and shared victories.

The once dreaded office potlucks had become a celebration of their diversity, each individual bringing their own unique flavor to the table, both literally and figuratively. The drama queen, once a source of constant agitation, had found her voice in constructive criticism, channeling her passion for gossip into valuable insights about team dynamics. The procrastinator, now a champion of last-minute inspiration, had discovered the power of deadlines, using them as fuel for bursts of creativity that surprised even himself.

The office's new vision was a tapestry woven from their individual strengths and shared experiences. They had learned to embrace their differences, realizing that their unique perspectives were not obstacles to overcome, but rather assets to be celebrated. The office had become a microcosm of the wider world, a space where individuality was valued and collaboration was the key to success.

This newfound harmony wasn't a utopia, however. They still had their moments of friction, their disagreements, and their occasional bouts of frustration. But they had learned to approach these challenges with a newfound level of understanding and respect. They had learned that conflict was not the enemy, but rather an opportunity for growth, as long as it was navigated with grace and humor.

One afternoon, as the team gathered around the now-organized coffee machine for their daily caffeine ritual, the topic of their future plans came up. The conversation flowed effortlessly, punctuated by bursts of laughter and shared dreams. They had tackled the chaos of their past and were ready to embrace the exciting possibilities that lay ahead.

"Remember when we thought we were doomed?" Sarah, the former drama queen, chuckled, taking a sip of her latte. "We were drowning in piles of paperwork, gossip, and procrastination, and all we could do was laugh."

"Ah, those were the days," David, the notorious procrastinator, chimed in with a twinkle in his eye. "Remember the time I managed to submit a report a whole day late, and somehow still managed to get a promotion?"

The room erupted in laughter, a collective memory of their chaotic past. It was a reminder of how far they had come, a testament to the resilience and humor that had gotten them through the toughest times.

"We're not just colleagues anymore," said Emily, the quiet observer who had been the glue that held the team together. "We're a team. We've been through the trenches together, and we've emerged stronger on the other side."

"Indeed," added Michael, the ever-optimistic leader who had seen the potential in each of them. "We've created a workplace where we can be ourselves, where we can support each other, and where we can achieve great things together."

The conversation continued, their shared vision taking shape as they discussed their future goals. They dreamed of launching innovative projects, achieving ambitious milestones, and becoming a beacon of collaboration and creativity within their company.

As the afternoon sun streamed through the office windows, casting warm rays on their faces, a sense of optimism filled the air. They had faced the wreckage, embraced the chaos, and emerged as a unified force, ready to navigate the future together, with laughter, determination, and a shared vision that had transformed them from colleagues to a team.

Their journey had been a testament to the power of human connection, the importance of laughter in the face of adversity, and the transformative power of embracing one's quirks and flaws. They had learned that the most chaotic situations could be navigated with a little bit of humor, a lot of teamwork, and a shared vision for a better future.

And as the team left the office that evening, their footsteps echoed with a newfound sense of purpose, a reflection of their collective journey from the wreckage to a future brimming with possibility. They had wrangled the wreckage, and in doing so, they had discovered the power of their own collective spirit.

The Power of Collaboration

The office, once a swirling vortex of misplaced staplers, forgotten deadlines, and whispered gossip, had finally found its footing. The constant cacophony of "Where's my coffee mug?" and "Who ate the last donut?" had been replaced by a surprisingly harmonious hum of focused effort. It was a transformation orchestrated by the collective will of individuals who had once viewed each other as adversaries, now bound together by a shared understanding: chaos was the enemy, and teamwork their only weapon.

Remember Kevin, the chronic procrastinator, whose life revolved around the thrilling adrenaline rush of last-minute deadlines? He was now a beacon of productivity, his desk a testament to his newfound organizational prowess. It was a sight to behold, like witnessing a hummingbird transform into a meticulous accountant. The office drama queen, Brenda, whose whispers had once fueled the flames of office discontent, had discovered the joy of constructive collaboration. Instead of gossiping about the new intern's questionable fashion choices, she now used her knack for gathering information to propose innovative ideas for streamlining their workflow.

The power of collaboration, once a concept relegated to motivational posters and corporate retreats, had finally become a tangible reality. It was a revelation that came not through forced team-building exercises or mandatory leadership seminars, but through the shared struggles and triumphs of navigating a workplace in crisis. The office was no longer a battlefield of passive-aggressive sticky notes and stolen lunches; it had become a haven of mutual support and understanding.

The transformation wasn't without its hurdles. There were moments of frustration, setbacks, and the occasional misplaced memo. Yet, amidst the challenges, a spirit of unity had emerged. The office had rediscovered the value of diverse perspectives, realizing that even the most chaotic personalities could contribute something unique to the collective effort.

The once-dreaded team meetings had become a platform for open communication, where ideas were exchanged, concerns were addressed, and laughter was shared. It was during these meetings that the true power of collaboration blossomed. By pooling their individual strengths and weaknesses, the team began to achieve what no single individual could have accomplished on their own.

One of the most compelling examples of this collaborative power emerged during the office's annual fundraiser. In the past, this event had been a logistical nightmare, a symphony of miscommunication and half-baked ideas. But this year, with the newfound spirit of unity, the team embraced the challenge with gusto. They pooled their resources, brainstorming ideas, and devising strategies that leveraged each individual's unique talents. Brenda, with her flair for theatrics, spearheaded the marketing campaign, creating a series of hilarious social media posts that generated a wave of interest and engagement. Kevin, with his meticulous attention to detail, managed the logistics, ensuring that every aspect of the event was meticulously planned and executed. The once-dreaded fundraising event became a resounding success, not only surpassing their financial goals but also forging stronger bonds within the team.

The power of collaboration extended beyond the office walls. It permeated every aspect of their lives, from volunteering at a local soup kitchen to organizing a neighborhood block party. The team, once a collection of isolated individuals, had become a force for good, using their collective strengths to make a positive impact on their community.

However, the journey wasn't always a smooth sailing. There were moments of doubt, moments when the weight of responsibility threatened to overwhelm them. But they persevered, reminding themselves of the progress they had made, the bonds they had forged, and the power of their collective spirit.

The office, once a symbol of chaos and disarray, had become a testament to the transformative power of collaboration. It was a reminder that even in the most tumultuous environments, unity could emerge, and dreams could be realized. The journey was far from over, but the team was ready to navigate the future together, their collective strength guiding them towards a brighter horizon.

The power of collaboration wasn't just a buzzword or a management trend; it was a force that could reshape individuals, transform workplaces, and inspire communities. And in the end, it was the shared journey, the laughter, the frustrations, and the triumphs that made this journey so meaningful. It was a reminder that even in the most chaotic of situations, the human spirit could prevail, fueled by the power of unity and the shared pursuit of a common goal.

Embracing Diversity

The office had become a melting pot of personalities, each with their unique quirks and talents. It was a vibrant mix of introverts and extroverts, analytical minds and creative souls, meticulous planners and free-spirited improvisers. This diversity, initially perceived as a source of chaos, was now recognized as the team's greatest strength.

It had been a long and winding road, marked by numerous mishaps, near-meltdowns, and a fair share of laughter. The office had been a stage for the drama queen's grand pronouncements, the procrastinator's last-minute scrambles, and the meticulous planner's exasperated sighs. However, amidst the turmoil, a remarkable transformation had taken place. The team had discovered that their differences were not a liability, but a source of ingenuity and resilience.

The analytical minds had brought structure and order to their projects, while the creative souls had injected innovative ideas and fresh perspectives. The meticulous planners had ensured deadlines were met, while the free-spirited improvisers had found solutions to unexpected challenges. It was this harmonious blend of personalities that had allowed the team to weather the storm and emerge stronger than ever.

The team's journey had taught them the value of embracing diversity, not just in terms of personality, but also in their skill sets and perspectives. They had come to appreciate the fact that each individual brought something unique to the table, contributing to the collective success.

The office, once a battlefield of conflicting approaches, had become a canvas for collaboration and shared purpose. Team members learned to leverage their differences, recognizing that their diverse strengths created a powerful synergy. It was a symphony of individual talents, harmonizing to create a beautiful and efficient work environment.

They had learned to appreciate the power of perspective, understanding that different viewpoints could enrich their problem-solving abilities. The analytical minds could dissect problems, breaking them down into manageable components, while the creative souls could envision innovative solutions that defied conventional thinking.

The team's journey had also taught them the importance of empathy and understanding. They had learned to navigate disagreements with compassion and respect, valuing each other's contributions, even when they disagreed. They had learned to listen to each other's perspectives, acknowledging the value of diverse thoughts and experiences.

The office, once a place of whispers and gossip, had become a space for open communication and honest feedback. Team members had learned to express their opinions respectfully, valuing the feedback of their colleagues. They had learned to embrace constructive criticism, recognizing its potential to elevate their work and foster individual growth.

This newfound respect for diversity extended beyond personality traits and skills. The team embraced the rich tapestry of cultures and backgrounds represented within their ranks. They had learned to celebrate the nuances of different communication styles, perspectives, and experiences. This cultural awareness had fostered a sense of inclusion and belonging, creating a welcoming and supportive work environment for everyone.

The team had discovered that embracing diversity wasn't just about tolerance, it was about celebrating the richness and complexity that came with it. They had learned to value the unique perspectives and experiences that each member brought to the table, recognizing that it was these very differences that made the team stronger, more innovative, and more adaptable.

As they looked to the future, the team was brimming with optimism and a shared sense of purpose. They knew that the challenges ahead would be formidable, but they were confident in their ability to navigate them together, fueled by the power of collaboration and the strength of their diverse team. The journey had been transformative, not just for the office, but for each individual member. They had learned to embrace the beauty of their differences, recognizing that true success was born from unity and a celebration of individuality.

Celebrating Differences

The office, once a breeding ground for chaos and passive-aggressive sticky notes, had begun to resemble a surprisingly well-oiled machine. The air no longer vibrated with the hum of discontent; instead, it buzzed with a newfound sense of camaraderie and shared purpose. The once-dreaded Monday mornings, once dreaded for their promise of another week of organizational nightmares, now held a hint of optimism. This was a testament to the power of embracing differences, not as obstacles, but as unique strengths that, when combined, could propel the team towards a brighter future.

One sunny afternoon, as the office team gathered for their weekly "Wrangle the Wreckage" meeting, a sense of quiet accomplishment hung in the air. This wasn't the same meeting that had been dominated by panicked whispers about deadlines missed and presentations sabotaged. Instead, it was a space for celebrating wins, however small, and acknowledging the unique contributions each member brought to the table.

Sarah, the resident procrastinator, whose penchant for last-minute sprints had once been the bane of their existence, was now being commended for her ability to think outside the box and generate innovative solutions under pressure. Her ability to work effectively under tight deadlines, once viewed as a liability, was now seen as a valuable asset.

Mark, the former office gossip, whose penchant for spreading whispers had created more than a few workplace dramas, had, in a surprising turn of events, become the team's resident connector. His ability to sniff out information and navigate the office's social currents was now channeled into building bridges and fostering collaboration. The office, once a breeding ground for rumors and whispers, was now a hub for productive discussions and collaborative problem-solving.

David, the office perfectionist, who had once been a stickler for rules and regulations, now embraced the team's creative energy. He recognized that while structure was important, a little bit of chaos could spark innovation and lead to unexpected breakthroughs. He had even been known to suggest a "no-rules" brainstorming session, a proposition that would have been met with horrified gasps just a few weeks ago.

The team's newfound appreciation for each other's unique strengths was a testament to the power of embracing diversity. They had learned that their differences, far from being obstacles, were actually the very ingredients that made their team so effective. They had learned to celebrate each other's quirks, to see their flaws as opportunities for growth, and to recognize that a little bit of chaos, in the right hands, could be a powerful force for good.

But it wasn't just about celebrating individual differences; it was also about understanding that these differences could be leveraged to create a truly cohesive and effective team. The office, once a collection of individuals struggling to navigate their own chaotic agendas, was now a symphony of diverse talents working in harmony to achieve a shared vision.

Their weekly meetings had become a testament to this newfound harmony. They no longer simply dealt with the fallout of individual mishaps. Instead, they brainstormed as a team, each member contributing their unique perspective to the conversation. They learned to listen to each other, to respect dissenting opinions, and to find solutions that took into account the needs of everyone. This wasn't just about collaboration; it was about creating a space where each member felt heard, valued, and empowered.

One of the most remarkable transformations was the office's approach to problem-solving. Once, a problem would be met with a flurry of individual attempts to fix it, often resulting in a patchwork of conflicting solutions. Now, the team approached problems collaboratively, pooling their resources and brainstorming together. This collaborative approach, fueled by the team's newfound respect for each other's abilities, resulted in innovative and effective solutions that wouldn't have been possible if they had remained siloed in their individual worlds.

The team's journey wasn't always smooth sailing. There were still moments of tension, misunderstandings, and the occasional outburst of frustration. But the difference was that they now had the tools, the trust, and the shared vision to navigate these challenges effectively. They had learned to communicate openly, to resolve conflicts constructively, and to support each other through difficult times.

This ability to navigate the inevitable bumps in the road with grace and resilience was a testament to the strength they had found in their diversity. They had learned that differences weren't weaknesses; they were the very source of their resilience. They had learned that by celebrating their differences, they were not only creating a more productive and effective team, but they were also building a stronger, more supportive, and more resilient community within their workplace.

As the team sat together, their faces glowing with the satisfaction of a job well done, they realized that their journey had not only transformed their work environment, but it had also transformed them as individuals. They had emerged from the chaos, not as survivors, but as stronger, more connected, and more capable individuals. They had learned to embrace their differences, not just as individuals, but as a team. They had learned to wrangle the wreckage, not by crushing it, but by building something beautiful and strong out of the pieces.

And as they looked toward the future, they did so with a sense of confidence and shared purpose. They knew that they were not just a group of individuals working side-by-side; they were a team, a community united by their shared vision and their unwavering belief in the power of their diversity. The future, once filled with the specter of chaos and uncertainty, now shimmered with the promise of new adventures, new challenges, and new opportunities to build something extraordinary together.

The Journey Continues

The air in the office crackled with a newfound energy. The once-familiar whispers of discontent had been replaced by a symphony of laughter, a chorus of collaboration, and the gentle hum of productivity. It was as if a magical spell had been cast, transforming the once chaotic landscape into a haven of teamwork and shared purpose.

The team had come a long way. They'd faced their demons, confronted their quirks, and learned to embrace the beautiful chaos that was their collective work identity. From the procrastinator who'd discovered the joy of deadlines to the drama queen who'd finally found her voice in constructive criticism, they'd all found their place within the harmonious rhythm of the office.

Their journey had been a testament to the power of unity. They'd learned that even the most dysfunctional of teams could find solace in shared laughter, a sense of belonging, and the unwavering support of their peers.

Now, with the storm clouds of disarray behind them, they looked forward to a future filled with optimism and adventure. They were no longer simply colleagues; they were a family, united by their shared experiences, their resilience, and their enduring sense of humor.

The office was no longer a battlefield, but a playground. Their shared vision for the future was crystal clear: to continue their journey, to face new challenges with unwavering optimism, to celebrate their unique quirks, and to embrace the exhilarating symphony of their collective strengths.

The team embraced the ever-changing landscape of the
office, knowing that even the most unexpected twists and
turns could be navigated with grace, humor, and a dash of
camaraderie. They were a testament to the fact that even in
the most chaotic of workplaces, the human spirit, fueled by
laughter and a shared sense of purpose, could create a haven
of harmony and success.

The future held endless possibilities, and they were ready to
face them head-on, armed with their newfound unity, their
collective wit, and an unshakeable belief in their ability to
wrangle the wreckage, one chaotic challenge at a time.

The once-dreaded Monday mornings now ushered in a wave
of excitement. The office hummed with the energy of a team
on the cusp of greatness, ready to unleash their potential and
forge a new era of collaboration and success.

Their journey was far from over. New challenges would
emerge, new obstacles would test their resilience, but they
were no longer afraid. They had conquered chaos, embraced
change, and discovered the power of a united front. They
were a team, a family, ready to face whatever the future held,
together.

Their shared experience had taught them that the most
effective weapon against chaos wasn't a rigid system or a
rule-bound approach, but a shared sense of humor, a
willingness to learn from mistakes, and a deep understanding
of the unique strengths that each member brought to the
table.

They were a testament to the fact that even in the most
unconventional of workplaces, a little laughter, a lot of
empathy, and an unwavering commitment to teamwork

could transform a chaotic landscape into a haven of productivity, purpose, and shared success.

The journey continued, and with each passing day, they grew stronger, wiser, and more determined to navigate the future together, armed with their shared experiences, their unique strengths, and a whole lot of laughter along the way.

The Final Showdown

The office buzzed with a strange energy, a mix of nervous anticipation and a giddy sense of accomplishment. The air, usually thick with the scent of stale coffee and forgotten lunches, now carried a whiff of triumph. It was the culmination of months of wrangling, scheming, and, yes, even laughter. The team had survived the storm, navigating treacherous waters of procrastination, gossip, and a whole lot of office drama.

Their final showdown, a project so complex it had the potential to sink the entire ship, was upon them. The pressure was immense, a whirlwind of deadlines, expectations, and the weight of their collective anxieties. But as they huddled together, a sense of unity, forged through shared struggles, emerged. Their leader, a wise old soul named Harold, had a knack for turning chaos into opportunity.

"Remember, folks," Harold declared, his voice booming through the room, "we've already waded through the muck of office politics. We've learned to laugh at ourselves, to appreciate the absurdity of it all. Now, we're going to show them what we're really capable of. Let's finish this with a flourish!"

Their plan, a masterpiece of strategic brilliance, was set in motion. They divided tasks, utilizing each individual's strengths. The procrastinator, now a reformed soul, surprised everyone with his meticulous attention to detail. The drama queen, humbled by her past actions, channeled her passion into creative solutions. And the rest of the team, their differences now a source of strength, worked seamlessly together.

It wasn't easy. Deadlines loomed, challenges surfaced, and the occasional panic attack threatened to derail their progress. But they persevered, their laughter, a powerful weapon against the onslaught of stress, echoing through the office. They faced the looming deadline with an infectious optimism, fueled by the realization that they were more than just co-workers; they were a team.

The final presentation, a nerve-wracking spectacle, began. Each team member delivered their part with confidence and passion, their individual talents blending into a harmonious symphony of success. As they concluded, a collective sigh of relief swept through the room.

Their manager, a stern woman known for her demanding nature, had a rare look of approval on her face. "Well done," she declared, a hint of surprise in her voice. "You've proven that teamwork, dedication, and a little bit of laughter can overcome any obstacle."

The office erupted in cheers, the victory sweeter for all the challenges they had faced. They had wrangled the wreckage, transforming their workplace into a haven of collaboration and camaraderie. They had learned that even the most disorganized office could be a place of growth, laughter, and unexpected triumphs.

The journey was far from over. The office would always have its share of quirks, its moments of chaos, and its inherent absurdity. But now, with a renewed sense of purpose and a shared understanding of their strengths, the team was ready to tackle any challenge that came their way. They had discovered that laughter was not just a coping mechanism; it was a source of resilience, innovation, and, most importantly, a reminder that even in the most chaotic of workplaces, there was always room for joy.

As the final project wrapped up, a sense of satisfaction filled the air. The office had undergone a transformation, evolving from a place of disarray into a harmonious ecosystem. They had wrangled the wreckage, turning their struggles into a testament to the power of collaboration, laughter, and the enduring spirit of those who dared to turn chaos into a symphony of success.

The story of their journey was a reminder that even the most disorganized office can be a place of growth, laughter, and unexpected triumphs. It was a celebration of the human spirit, a testament to the power of teamwork, and a reminder that, sometimes, the best way to face chaos is with a smile and a good dose of humor.

Culmination of Efforts

The office had become a battlefield of crumpled papers, half-eaten lunches, and the lingering scent of desperation. We were a team of once-peaceful professionals, now reduced to a band of misfits grappling with the wreckage of our own bad habits. It wasn't supposed to be this way. We had all dreamed of a harmonious office, a haven of productivity, and most importantly, a place where our colleagues wouldn't drive us to the brink of madness. But somewhere along the way, the chaos had taken over, and the once-organized chaos had become… well, just chaos.

We had tried everything. We had devised intricate schemes, implemented clever tactics, and even resorted to a little bit of sabotage (don't worry, all in good fun). We had gone from friendly colleagues to conspirators, plotting and scheming, all in the name of reclaiming our sanity. But our efforts, despite their valiant intentions, had only led to further disarray.

Remember the time we attempted to replace the office coffee machine with a self-cleaning, self-brewing miracle of modern technology? It ended with a lukewarm, metallic-tasting brew and an office-wide panic as everyone scrambled for their own private stash of coffee. Or the time we decided to implement a "no-email-after-6pm" policy, only to find ourselves bombarded with an avalanche of unread emails the next morning?

It was like the universe itself was conspiring against us, throwing us curveballs at every turn. Yet, through the laughter, the frustration, and the occasional caffeine-fueled meltdown, we began to see a glimmer of hope.

It started with the procrastinator, once a master of last-minute mayhem. He had always viewed the office as a giant game, a test of his ability to pull off the impossible. But somewhere along the way, he realized that his constant late nights and frenzied deadlines were actually hurting everyone. He started taking on smaller tasks, completing them before they turned into monstrous obligations. He even volunteered to help with the company's annual charity drive, proving that his chaos had a heart of gold.

And then there was the drama queen, the purveyor of gossip, the source of office-wide anxiety. Her tendency to embellish the truth and turn every minor mishap into a full-blown crisis had created a toxic atmosphere. But after facing the consequences of her actions, she had a change of heart. She realized that her need to be the center of attention was hindering the team's progress and instead of fueling the flames of drama, she started focusing on building real connections with her colleagues.

The most surprising transformation, however, was in the most unlikely of characters: the office's silent observer, the person who seemed to be immune to the chaos that surrounded us. They had always remained detached, observing the carnage from a safe distance, but when the office's fate hung in the balance, they stepped forward. They offered solutions, calmed anxieties, and even volunteered to take over the company's social media accounts, which were notoriously difficult to manage.

Our efforts were beginning to pay off. The air was no longer filled with the tension of imminent deadlines and the whispers of rumors. We were a team, united by a common goal, a desire to reclaim our office from the clutches of chaos. The crumpled papers were being neatly filed, the half-eaten lunches were finding their way to the trash, and the scent of desperation was being replaced by the hopeful aroma of freshly brewed coffee.

We had a long way to go, but we were finally on the right track. And we knew that even when the next round of chaos inevitably hit, we would be ready. We had learned that in the face of the absurd, the ridiculous, and the utterly chaotic, the power of laughter, teamwork, and a good cup of coffee could conquer all.

But the journey to a truly organized and efficient office wasn't always smooth sailing. There were still those days when we were bombarded with emails, lost in a maze of paperwork, and left wondering if we were ever truly going to escape the chaos. But as we navigated the treacherous waters of workplace disarray, we discovered a newfound strength within ourselves. We learned that even in the most chaotic situations, a little bit of humor and a lot of teamwork could go a long way.

And we learned something even more profound. We realized that the most unexpected heroes often rise from the midst of the chaos. We saw that the procrastinator, once a symbol of last-minute pandemonium, could become the most reliable team player. We witnessed how the drama queen, known for her gossiping tendencies, could blossom into a valued team member. And we discovered that even the most silent observer could become the office's most influential voice.

It wasn't about changing who we were, but about embracing our unique quirks and personalities. We had learned to appreciate our differences, to embrace our weaknesses, and to find strength in our shared vulnerabilities. We had become more than just colleagues; we had become a team, a family, bound together by a shared desire for a more harmonious and productive work environment.

And as we stood there, amidst the newly organized office, surrounded by colleagues who were now more like friends, we realized that the journey to overcome chaos was not just about restoring order. It was about finding common ground, celebrating differences, and building a workplace where everyone could thrive. It was about turning our office into a place where we could all laugh, learn, and grow, together.

The culmination of our efforts was a symphony of sorts, a harmonious blend of laughter, teamwork, and a shared sense of accomplishment. The chaos had been wrangled, the wreckage had been cleared, and we had emerged from the battle stronger, wiser, and more connected than ever before. And as we looked to the future, we knew that even if a new wave of chaos were to crash down upon us, we would be ready to face it head-on. We had learned to navigate the unpredictable tides of workplace disarray, and we had discovered that in the face of adversity, humor and teamwork could always prevail.

We were a team of wranglers, united in our commitment to a more organized and efficient workplace. And we knew that no matter what challenges lay ahead, we would face them together. Because we had learned that in the wild, unpredictable world of office life, the only way to survive was to laugh, learn, and grow together.

The Humor Factor Revisited

As the dust settled from their final showdown, a wave of relief washed over the office. The chaos they had weathered, the schemes they had hatched, the laughter they had shared – it all culminated in this moment of hard-earned triumph. The once-fractured team had emerged stronger, their bonds forged in the crucible of shared adversity.

But amidst the euphoria, a sobering truth lingered: their journey hadn't been a smooth one. It was a testament to their collective resilience that they had managed to navigate the treacherous waters of workplace disarray, finding humor in the most unexpected places. It was a stark reminder that in the face of chaos, a good laugh could be the ultimate weapon.

Humor, they discovered, wasn't just a lighthearted escape from the daily grind; it was a potent tool for building bridges and fostering unity. It served as a common language, bridging the gaps between personalities as different as the planets themselves. Remember the chronic procrastinator, the office drama queen? They were, in a strange way, perfect partners in crime, their shared love for chaos inadvertently bringing them together.

And what about the office's resident comedian? They were the unsung heroes, their witticisms acting as a balm for the soul, their jokes defusing tension before it could escalate into a full-blown meltdown. They were the silent orchestrators of harmony, reminding everyone that laughter, even in the most stressful situations, could be a powerful force for good.

Take, for instance, the infamous "Great Coffee Machine Caper." The office's ancient coffee machine, affectionately nicknamed "The Beast," had a penchant for malfunctioning, leaving its users stranded with nothing but lukewarm, bitter water to fuel their day. It was a situation ripe for frustration, a breeding ground for office meltdowns.

But the team, with their newfound camaraderie, decided to embrace the challenge. They turned the coffee crisis into an opportunity for creative collaboration, a testament to their ability to find humor even in the most dire of circumstances. The procrastinator, armed with a caffeine-fueled burst of inspiration, concocted a plan to bribe the office janitor with a stack of freshly baked cookies in exchange for "a little extra attention" for the machine.

The drama queen, surprisingly, joined in the effort, offering her expertise in the art of "subtle persuasion," using a series of carefully crafted emails that subtly hinted at the dire consequences of a coffee-less office. Their efforts, albeit unconventional, were surprisingly effective.

"The Beast" roared back to life, spewing forth gallons of steaming hot coffee, the aroma filling the air with the promise of a caffeinated utopia. It was a victory that felt as sweet as the cookies that had fueled their success.

And so, the office learned a valuable lesson. It was a lesson that transcended the petty squabbles, the endless email threads, and the endless stream of office gossip. It was a lesson that revealed the power of humor to mend fences, to bridge divides, to bring a team together.

For in the end, it was the ability to find humor in the mundane, the absurd, the downright chaotic that truly made the difference. They realized that embracing laughter, even in the face of adversity, was not only a way to survive the madness of the office, but a way to truly thrive. They learned that humor was the glue that held their team together, the secret weapon that allowed them to not just wrangle the wreckage, but transform it into something beautiful.

And as they sat there, amidst the remnants of their collective chaos, a collective chuckle rippled through the room. It was a sound that spoke of resilience, of camaraderie, of the transformative power of laughter in the face of adversity. They were, after all, the Wranglers of Wreckage, a team united by a shared love of humor and a shared determination to overcome any obstacle that came their way.

The story of their transformation was one that would be told and retold, a cautionary tale and a celebration of resilience, a reminder that even the most chaotic of offices could find harmony, one laughter-filled moment at a time. The office was no longer just a place where they worked, it was a place where they laughed, where they learned, where they truly belonged. And it was all thanks to the magic of humor.

Resolution and Growth

The office buzzed with an energy unlike anything they'd
experienced before. The air, usually thick with the scent of
stale coffee and forgotten dreams, now carried the tang of
triumph and the sweet aroma of accomplishment. It had been
a long, winding road, paved with crumpled deadlines, broken
promises, and enough office drama to rival a Shakespearean
tragedy. But through it all, they had emerged, battered but
unbowed, a team forged in the fires of chaos, a testament to
the power of laughter and the enduring strength of
camaraderie.

The source of this newfound vitality was the epic
showdown, a battle that had pitted them against the very
essence of office inefficiency, against the forces of
procrastination, gossip, and the tyranny of the inbox. The
culmination of their efforts had been a week-long sprint of
organization, a mad dash to tame the beast of disarray that
had threatened to swallow them whole. They had wrestled
with overflowing filing cabinets, waded through mountains
of paperwork, and even faced the daunting task of organizing
the office supply closet, a place where time itself seemed to
bend and twist.

The journey had been arduous, a chaotic dance of missed
deadlines, impromptu meetings, and the inevitable coffee
spills that punctuated the rhythm of their frantic days. But
through it all, a sense of unity had emerged, a shared purpose
that transcended the individual quirks and idiosyncrasies that
had once defined them. They had learned to embrace the
chaos, not as an enemy to be vanquished, but as a catalyst
for change, a crucible in which they could forge a stronger

sense of self and a deeper connection to their fellow colleagues.

The procrastinator, once a master of last-minute miracles, had discovered a newfound sense of urgency, fueled by a sense of responsibility that he never knew he possessed. He had embraced the power of lists, the discipline of deadlines, and the sheer joy of crossing off tasks on his to-do list, a ritual that had become his personal mantra, his guiding light in the darkness of procrastination. The office drama queen, once a whirlwind of gossip and intrigue, had found solace in the shared purpose, in the camaraderie that transcended the petty squabbles and the drama that had once consumed her days. She discovered the power of empathy, the importance of listening, and the true meaning of friendship, qualities that had been buried beneath the layers of gossip and manipulation.

Their journey had been a crash course in the art of communication, a masterclass in the power of collaboration. They had learned to articulate their needs, to listen with empathy, and to negotiate with grace, forging a new language of understanding that transcended the walls of their individual silos. They had learned the power of humor, its ability to defuse tension, to bridge divides, and to remind them that even in the face of chaos, there was always room for a chuckle, a shared joke, a moment of levity.

The office, once a battlefield of missed deadlines and miscommunication, had been transformed into a haven of productivity, a space where ideas flowed freely, where collaboration thrived, and where the laughter of colleagues filled the air like a soothing balm. The final showdown had been a triumph, a testament to their collective resilience, a reminder that even in the midst of chaos, there was always hope, always the possibility of redemption, always the chance to wrangle the wreckage and emerge victorious.

But the journey had not been without its scars. They had learned to navigate the treacherous terrain of office politics, to decipher the subtle cues and the unspoken rules that governed their daily lives. They had faced the temptation to succumb to the allure of gossip, to indulge in the petty drama that seemed to be an inevitable part of the workplace. But they had resisted, choosing instead to build bridges, to foster understanding, and to create a culture of respect and mutual support.

The final showdown was not just a victory over their office woes, but a victory over themselves, a testament to their growth, a reminder of the power of resilience. They had discovered that the true meaning of success lay not in the perfection of their organization, but in the strength of their bonds, in their shared commitment to a better future, and in their unwavering belief in the power of laughter to heal and to unite.

And as the office settled into its new normal, a sense of quiet satisfaction settled upon them, a sense of accomplishment that went beyond the tidy desks and the organized files. They had wrestled with the wreckage of their past, faced the demons of their own disorganization, and emerged stronger, wiser, and more united than ever before. They had wrangled the wreckage, and in the process, they had discovered the true meaning of teamwork, the enduring power of camaraderie, and the magic of finding laughter in the midst of chaos.

A Triumphant Ending

The air crackled with a mix of anticipation and nervous energy. After weeks of chaos, strategic planning, and the occasional misplaced stapler, the team finally stood on the precipice of victory. Their final challenge, a colossal spreadsheet that threatened to engulf their entire existence, had been staring them down for weeks, its rows and columns a menacing labyrinth. But as the final edits were made, the team felt a sense of accomplishment wash over them.

The office buzzed with activity, a stark contrast to the quiet days of despair that had once dominated their existence. The procrastinator, who had once thrived on the brink of disaster, was now the calmest person in the room, his mind laser-focused on ensuring every comma was in its rightful place. The drama queen, who had once fueled office rumors with the speed of a wildfire, was now diligently cross-checking figures, her gossipy instincts redirected to the noble pursuit of accuracy.

As the spreadsheet finally reached completion, a collective sigh of relief echoed through the room. The team had conquered the chaos, not by brute force, but by harnessing the power of teamwork, humor, and the occasional shared coffee break. It was a victory that celebrated the unique blend of personalities that made their office so special.

The celebrations, of course, were nothing short of chaotic. There were impromptu dance parties, a spirited debate about the best way to celebrate (a pizza party or a karaoke night), and a hilarious attempt at a victory song that ended in a tangled mess of limbs and laughter. But even amidst the chaos, there was a sense of warmth and camaraderie, a feeling that they had accomplished something extraordinary.

As the laughter faded and the team settled into a newfound peace, they realized something profound. They had not just conquered the chaos, they had transformed it. The office was no longer a battlefield of mismatched priorities and miscommunication, it was a space where laughter, empathy, and shared goals thrived.

The once-dreaded spreadsheet now stood as a testament to their resilience, a physical manifestation of the journey they had taken together. It wasn't just a collection of numbers; it was a story, a story of their shared triumphs, their collective wisdom, and the power of human connection.

As the sun set on the office, casting long shadows across the desks and filing cabinets, they knew that the journey was far from over. There would always be new challenges, new messes to wrangle. But they were ready. They had learned to face the chaos, to embrace the humor, and to find strength in their shared experience.

And as they walked out of the office, the weight of their accomplishments settling over them, they knew that the chaos, while unpredictable, was ultimately a source of growth. It was a constant reminder of their ability to rise above adversity, to find unity in their differences, and to ultimately create a workplace where laughter and productivity intertwined. It was, in its own unique way, a triumph.

Acknowledgments

First and foremost, I want to express my deepest gratitude to my editor, Rebecca D' Enterprise, for their unwavering support, insightful feedback, and ability to keep my writing from veering into the realm of pure chaos.

To my friends and family, thank you for being the most supportive, patient, and understanding audience a writer could ask for. Your laughter, encouragement, and occasional eye rolls fueled this book to its completion.

A special shoutout to the countless office workers who have graced my path over the years. You, with your quirky habits and occasional bouts of utter disorganization, have provided an endless supply of inspiration. May you all find your inner Wrangle the Wreckage champion.

Appendix

This book wouldn't be complete without a collection of useful tools for conquering office chaos.

The "Wrangle the Wreckage" Checklist: A handy list of actionable steps to help you tame your workspace and regain control.

"Disorganized to Organized" 101: A guide to common office pitfalls and practical solutions to achieve a more productive and stress-free work environment.

The "Office Drama Survival Kit": A list of coping mechanisms and strategies for navigating the intricate world of office politics.

"The Procrastinator's Playbook": A step-by-step guide to turning procrastination into a valuable tool for creative problem-solving.

"The Gossip Queen's Code of Conduct": A set of guidelines for ethical communication and navigating the delicate balance of sharing information.

Glossary

Office Drama Queen: A person who thrives on creating and perpetuating office gossip and conflict.

Procrastination Champion: An individual who excels in the art of delaying tasks, often embracing chaos as a way of life.

Wrangle the Wreckage: The act of taking control of a chaotic situation and restoring order through humor and teamwork.

The "Humor Factor": The ability to find amusement in the midst of chaos and utilize laughter as a stress management tool.

Author Biography

Kandice Merrick is a humorist, workplace consultant, and business writer with a knack for finding the funny side of even the most chaotic situations. Having spent years navigating the treacherous waters of office politics, they decided to channel their experiences into a lighthearted guide to navigating the messy world of work. When not writing, they can be found indulging in their favorite pastimes - organizing their sock drawer, playing office-themed board games, and, of course, enjoying a good laugh.

218

- Acts of Kindness Tracker -

Kindness	Recipient	Completed

- Acts of Kindness Tracker -

Kindness	Recipient	Completed

- Acts of Kindness Tracker -

Kindness	Recipient	Completed

- Acts of Kindness Tracker -

Kindness	Recipient	Completed

www.ingramcontent.com/pod-product-compliance
Lightning Source LLC
Chambersburg PA
CBHW071934150726
47999CB00001B/204